The Matchless Six

The Story of Canada's First Women's Olympic Team

National Archives of Canada/PA151001

RON HOTCHKISS

Tundra Books

Published in Canada by Tundra Books,
75 Sherbourne Street, Toronto, Ontario M5A 2P9

Published in the United States by Tundra Books of Northern New York,
P.O. Box 1030, Plattsburgh, New York 12901

Library of Congress Control Number: 2005927007

Library and Archives Canada Cataloguing in Publication

Hotchkiss, Ron
    The matchless six : the story of Canada's first women's Olympic team / Ron Hotchkiss.

ISBN 0-88776-738-9

    1. Women athletes – Canada – History – 20th century – Juvenile literature.
2. Olympic Games (9th : 1928 : Amsterdam, Netherlands) – Juvenile literature.   I. Title.

GV709.18.C2H68 2006   j796.48'082'0971   C2005-902895-5

We acknowledge the financial support of the Government of Canada through the Book Publishing Industry Development Program (BPIDP) and that of the Government of Ontario through the Ontario Media Development Corporation's Ontario Book Initiative. We further acknowledge the support of the Canada Council for the Arts and the Ontario Arts Council for our publishing program.

ONTARIO ARTS COUNCIL
CONSEIL DES ARTS DE L'ONTARIO

Grateful acknowledgment is made to all those who have granted permission to reprint copyrighted and personal material. Every reasonable effort has been made to locate the copyright holders, but the publisher would welcome information that would allow them to rectify any omissions in future printings.

Photograph on title page: The Canadian women's Olympic team pose in their Olympic uniforms in Amsterdam: (first row, left to right) Ethel Smith, Myrtle Cook, Jean Thompson; (second row) Bobbie Rosenfeld, Ethel Catherwood, Jane Bell; (last row) Marie Parkes (chaperone), Bobby Kerr (coach), Alexandrine Gibb (manager).

Design: Sean Tai

ISBN 13: 978-0-88776-738-8
ISBN 10: 0-88776-738-9

Printed and bound in Canada

1 2 3 4 5 6   11 10 09 08 07 06

For my daughters, Megan and Caitlin

Contents

Author's Note

When young women began competing at athletic meets in Canada and the United States, they ran in distances measured by yards. For example, the events at the Canadian National Exhibition's Athletic Day included the 100 yards dash and the 4 x 110 yards relay. The field events of the high jump, broad jump, discus, javelin, and shot put, which came later, were measured in feet and inches. It wasn't until a competition held in Toronto on June 12, 1928, that metric measurements were first introduced. In this book, imperial measurements – yards, feet, inches – are used to reflect the standard of the time in which the women competed. To convert the imperial measurements to metric, use the following table.

One yard = 0.9144 meters

One foot = 0.3048 meters

One inch = 2.54 centimeters

Chapter One

The Canadian Women's Olympic Trials: Halifax, July 2, 1928

Myrtle Cook knew she had to be perfect. A poor start, a stumble along the way, or a failure to sustain the drive to the finish, all could spell disaster. There was no margin for error in the 100 meters, a race that separated winners from losers by a tenth of a second. Six years of athletic competition had taught her these hard lessons. Now, at Halifax's Wanderers Grounds on Dominion Day weekend, Myrtle faced the most important contest of her athletic life – the 100 meters final of the Canadian Women's Track-and-Field Championships and Olympic Trials. A national title was at stake, but so, too, was a place on the first Canadian women's team to compete at an Olympic Games. More than anything, Myrtle wanted to be a member of that team.

She had qualified for the final by winning her heat in 12⅕ seconds, which had bettered the world's record by a fifth of a second. The result boosted her confidence and made her the favorite to win the 100 meters. But she realized the other qualifiers were formidable opponents, capable of causing an upset. Bobbie Rosenfeld, the country's best all-round athlete, was one. Although Myrtle had beaten Rosenfeld at the Ontario Olympic Trials in Toronto ten days earlier, she knew Bobbie's ability and respected it. The same could be said of her friend and fellow member of the Canadian Ladies' Athletic Club,

Canada's Sports Hall of Fame

Myrtle Cook won the 100 meters at the Ontario Olympic Trials in only a fifth of a second over the world's record of 12²⁄₅ seconds. Here she is in the uniform of the Canadian Ladies' Athletic Club.

Ethel Smith, who had tied the old world's record in winning her heat. Eighteen-year-old Jane Bell was another who couldn't be taken lightly. Jane had something to prove in Halifax after her poor showing at the Ontario Trials. Earlier in the championships, she had set a new Canadian record for the 60 yards hurdles, a signal to watch out for her in the 100 meters.

As Myrtle took her place on the track and waited for the starter's commands, she was edgy. A highly strung athlete, she was nervous before every race. In her anxiety and hurry to get away at the beginning, she had acquired a dangerous habit as a sprinter: She tried to anticipate when the starter would fire his gun and break at that moment. Sometimes it worked, giving her that split-second advantage. Other times it didn't, resulting in a false start and a penalty. This race, however, was too important to risk. One break earned a warning, but two meant disqualification. She needed to wait for the sound of the gun.

"On your marks," commanded the starter.

Crouched at the line, feet firmly planted in her starting holes, Myrtle could feel the butterflies rising in her stomach. She tried to stay calm by focusing on the finish line, 100 meters down the track, willing her body to go fast and arrive there first.

"Get set."

She tensed, inhaled, and lifted her hips, ready to spring forward, determined that her world's record performance in qualifying wouldn't be undone by a loss in the final.

The pistol fired.

Her start was perfect. She broke quickly and sped away, head down and arms pumping. There was no faltering as she darted along the track. She could hear the other runners close behind, their spiked shoes hitting the cinder track. Yet there was no one in front of her. She could see the string at the finish coming nearer and, in a flash, she broke it and crossed the line in first place.

Following her, Jane was clearly fourth. The fight for second between Rosenfeld and Smith was close. The judges thought Bobbie was ahead at the end, but Ethel felt differently and so did the crowd. When the results were announced, the spectators began clapping their hands, stamping their feet, and hollering, "Twenty-three, twenty-three, twenty-three," which was Ethel's number. The reaction of the fans surprised her. Ethel could understand them rooting for a hometown girl, but she was a stranger from Toronto. Yet their protest had its effect. After a heated argument among the officials, the referee reversed the judges' decision, awarding Ethel second place.

The dispute was immediately forgotten when Myrtle's winning time was reported: It was 12 seconds, another world's record. The Wanderers Grounds erupted with cheers and applause. On the field she was surrounded by other athletes, offering their congratulations. Among them was Toronto teammate

At the Ontario Olympic Trials,
Ethel Smith placed second in the
100 meters.

Ethel Smith, who later telegraphed her mother the happy news: "MYRTLE
FIRST I SECOND FINAL TWELVE FLAT NEW WORLD'S RECORD."

Excited by Cook's performance, newspapermen praised her ability and
predicted great things. She was a wonderful performer, one said, having a
beautiful stride and terrific driving speed. Another declared that she would
show the world this swiftness at the Olympic Games in Amsterdam. A third
said she should win. For Myrtle Cook, encircled by well-wishers, cheers
from the crowd ringing in her ears, it was a thrilling moment. Selection to
the women's team assured, she could see the Olympics shining before her.

★

Because the high jump was the twelfth event on the program, Ethel Catherwood didn't begin competition until late in the afternoon. When she appeared, wearing the purple cape and matching purple top and shorts of the Parkdale Ladies' Athletic Club, the tall slim athlete was conspicuous. This was routine, for Ethel made an impression wherever she went. Her good looks had been well publicized, and those at the Wanderers Grounds who glimpsed her during the march-past of athletes in the opening ceremony weren't disappointed. Now, as Ethel walked across the field "like a princess making her debut before titled society," the crowd stirred.

A week earlier, a Halifax newspaper had announced that Ethel's athletic greatness needed no introduction to the sporting public of Nova Scotia. Since her debut at the Canadian Championships a year ago, where she set a national standard in the high jump and acquired the nickname the "Saskatoon Lily," interest in her had become widespread. As the best high jumper in the country, and no one to rival her, she was conceded a place on the Canadian Olympic Team. Before she left Toronto for the Olympic Trials, her friends predicted she would break her Canadian record. But Ethel was intent on achieving a loftier goal. A world's mark of 5 feet 3 inches, made by a South African girl in England, was recently reported. This was the incentive the Saskatoon athlete needed. She promised supporters, if the conditions were right, she would try to match it by exceeding her best jump of 5 feet 2⁷⁄₁₆ inches, made two years ago in Regina. Much

Author's collection

Ethel Catherwood, as the national record holder in the high jump, was assured a place on the Canadian Olympic Team. Here she is in the uniform of the Parkdale Ladies' Athletic Club.

was expected of her at the championships and, as she warmed up, all eyes were on her.

Her primary opponent would be sixteen-year-old Eva Dawes, a Toronto athlete and a former Canadian record holder. But Dawes had yet to clear 5 feet, a height Ethel found easy. It appeared there was no one to challenge the Saskatoon Lily. Yet this was neither the time nor the place to be complacent. These were the Olympic Trials, after all, and Ethel knew she needed to do her best. Walter Knox, her coach, was nearby as she jumped, observing her technique, providing advice, and offering encouragement. His presence and counsel helped as she soared over the bar with the grace of a bird. Her jumping had caught the fancy of the crowd, and each successful leap produced loud cheers and applause. Although Dawes cleared 5 feet for the first time, Ethel went three inches higher, winning the event and tying the world's record. The crossbar was raised to 5 feet 4 inches to give her the chance to be the world's record holder. After two failed attempts, however, she gave up and passed on a final try. A disappointed reporter felt that more effort would have carried her higher, but Ethel didn't care. She had won: Nothing else mattered.

When her winning height was announced, it produced a roar from the crowd that could be heard for many city blocks. Afterwards, admiring fans and defeated competitors gathered around her in celebration. Knox admitted Ethel had never jumped better, and was sure she could go five inches higher. She felt the same. "With more practise, I hope to better my mark made in this meet," she said.

A few minutes later, she returned to the field to compete in the javelin throw. Once more she thrilled the crowd by setting a record. She tossed the spear 118 feet 8 inches, breaking her Canadian mark of a year ago by over four feet. Her third-place finish in the discus seemed anticlimactic. A world's record tied and a Canadian one set were an impressive afternoon's work. She ended the day runner-up for the best athlete at the championships. In her hometown, the sports editor of the *Saskatoon Phoenix,* proud of her

Canada's best all-round female athlete, Bobbie Rosenfeld, was also the country's best discus thrower. She set a national mark of 108 feet 3¾ inches at the Ontario Olympic Trials.

performance, described her as "one of the greatest athletes in the Dominion." For the spectators at the Wanderers Grounds, it wasn't her athletic ability that left them buzzing, but her beauty and aloofness. She reigned over the field like the queen of a carnival, one reporter remarked, cool and unconcerned over victory.

If Ethel Catherwood regarded the competition with queenly indifference, Bobbie Rosenfeld was intensely combative. "She was aggressive, very aggressive physically," a contemporary remembered. "No, I don't mean that she made a lot of noise, or had a belligerent manner. She simply went after everything with full force." This was evident now as she executed her events in a no-nonsense fashion. She began the day by winning the shot put with a throw of 34 feet 11 inches. Moments later, jumping with a strength that gave male athletes a thing or two to think about, she set a national record in the running broad jump of 18 feet 3 inches. The qualifying heats for the 100 meters followed immediately and there was no time to rest. Nevertheless, her previous efforts in the shot put and broad jump seemed to have had little effect. She won her trial and finished third in the final, barely beaten out for second place. Realizing her best chance to make the Olympic team was in the discus throw, she withdrew from the 220 yards race. Bobbie then ended her competition as she began it: Taking the saucer-shaped object in her hand, flashing around on the balls of her feet, and sliding easily in the circle, she heaved the disc 120 feet 1 inch, shattering her Canadian mark by almost thirty-four feet, and coming within five feet of the world's record.

The crowd of 5,000 at the Wanderers Grounds watched Rosenfeld's exhibition of athletic prowess in amazement. In four hours, she won three of four events, setting Canadian records in two of them. She was a whole team in herself, and was crowned the meet's all-around champion. Those who knew her weren't surprised; to them, it was a typical Rosenfeld performance. But for the Maritimers that were seeing her in action for the first time, it was an outstanding display of talent and they were awed by the sight.

The sports editor of the *Halifax Chronicle* observed that few male athletes had her grace and all-around ability.

At first glance, there was nothing about the quiet teenager in the pale blue tracksuit that commanded attention. Lacking the style of a Rosenfeld or the glamor of a Catherwood, she seemed no different than most of the competitors at the championships. Yet her appearance was deceiving, and the high school student from Penetang, Ontario, arrived in Halifax heralded as a sure candidate for the Olympics. Not much older than most of the junior competitors at the championships, seventeen-year-old Jean Thompson had been unknown a month earlier. But at a warm-up meet for the Ontario Olympic Trials, and at the trials themselves, she had stunned onlookers by winning the 800 meters in close to world-record times. Lou Marsh, a sportswriter for the *Toronto Daily Star,* tagged her the "Penetanguishene Pansy." Yet the title belied her qualities as an athlete. A strong and clever runner, Jean had mastered a distance thought too much for a woman. At both competitions, she was so dominant that, like Catherwood, her selection to the team seemed certain. Still, many were curious to see how fast she would go in Halifax, hopeful she would set a world's mark.

Because of withdrawals, only one competitor, an athlete from Halifax's Ex-Dalhousie Ladies' Athletic Club, would face her in the 800 meters

Author's collection

The "boyish-bobbed" high-school girl from Penetang, Ontario, Jean Thompson was the star of the Ontario Olympic Trials in Toronto. She set a Canadian record in the 800 meters of 2 minutes 26 seconds.

Olympic Trial. The partisan throng was hopeful the local girl would prove a worthy opponent, perhaps upsetting the Penetang phenomenon. At the sound of the starter's pistol, the runners began two circuits of the track. Jean got off quickly, but her Halifax rival seemed equal to the challenge. Bolstered by the cheering of the 4,000 spectators encircling the race course and another 1,000 in the stands, the Maritimer stayed with the Ontario athlete for the first half, and it appeared anyone's race. Yet Jean was too strong and too experienced. In the second lap, she shook off her rival and pulled away, winning easily in 2 minutes 21⅕ seconds. It was believed she had broken the world's record. A report from Germany, however, indicated that a woman there had achieved a faster time. If true, Thompson was beaten out for the international mark. Still, her performance was noteworthy. In less than a month, she had lowered her time for the event by 9⅕ seconds and had set another Canadian record for the distance. Those who saw her run in Halifax were confident that it was only a matter of time before the world's record would be hers.

Following the final event, three members of the Women's Amateur Athletic Federation of Canada met to make an important decision. They were the selection committee responsible for picking the six representatives of the women's Olympic team. The squad would be chosen based on the results at the national Olympic Trials. Because of their performances, it seemed certain that Myrtle Cook, Ethel Smith, Jean Thompson, Ethel Catherwood, and Bobbie Rosenfeld would be five of the six selected. Who the final member would be was uncertain.

As she stood with the others, waiting for the selection committee's announcement, Jane Bell was nervous. All of the work and sacrifice of the past few months had come down to this one afternoon in Halifax and she wasn't hopeful. A few days before, Ted Reeve, a Toronto *Evening Telegram* sportswriter, tried to explain to his readers the importance of the trials to Olympic aspirants. He said that one good race at the right time, one long leap or extra-good heave and it was "ALL ABOARD FOR AMSTERDAM." But a few steps lost in the run, a few inches short in the jumps, and a slipup in the throw meant the bright dream of fame and travel gone. Jane knew that only the best would be taken to the Olympics. Her one good race had been the 60 yards hurdles, but it wasn't part of the Olympic program. Everything depended on her fourth-place finish in the 100 meters and she was discouraged. "I didn't think I would be on the team," she said. "I didn't think I was good enough."

Their deliberations over, the selection committee announced the names of those on the squad and their Olympic events – Myrtle Cook and Ethel Smith, 100 meters and relay; Ethel Catherwood, the running high jump; Bobbie Rosenfeld, the discus and relay; Jean Thompson, 800 meters and spare for the relay. Jane listened anxiously as the names were called. Finally, she heard, "Jane Bell, relay." She began jumping and yelling. "I was the only one who was really surprised," she said.

A few days later, it was discovered that the maximum number of entries allowed for individual track-and-field events at the Amsterdam Olympics was four instead of two. Jane and Bobbie were added to the 100 meters and were considered possible entrants for the 800 meters. Catherwood was a prospect for the discus.

In the days following the Halifax championships and Olympic Trials, local newspapers boasted the

Author's collection

Jane Bell hoped to be on the women's Olympic team, but a poor performance at the Ontario Trials hurt her chances. "She never knows when she is beaten," one sportswriter observed, "and will battle all the way."

meet was not only the greatest in the Maritimes in which women had competed, but the greatest athletic achievement in years. One paper declared that the events would go down in athletic history as one of the most impressive meets Canada had ever known, both from a competitive standpoint and enthusiasm displayed. The feats of the athletic stars from Ontario – who raced, jumped, and hurled to victory – were a marvel, another paper observed. No records were safe, it raved, no feats impossible. Their exhibitions of speed and strength at the championships were a revelation. "Had some of our male athletes also competed," a local sportswriter said, "it is doubtful if they would have defeated some of the so-called weaker sex."

Those who witnessed the display of athletic talent at the Wanderers Grounds came away convinced that Canada's female representatives would hold their own at the Olympics. They were certain that the Ontario sprinters were the best in the world, and wouldn't run second to anybody. The winners in Halifax would be world champions in Amsterdam.

A day after the meet, sportswriter Ted Reeve rhymed:

> *Myrtle and Smitty*
>   *And Fanny and Flo*
> *And Ethel and Jean*
>   *Are the girls that will go.*

As "the girls that will go," the six would be the first to compete for their country at a Summer Olympics, and the first Canadian women's team to participate at an Olympic Games. None of them were veteran track-and-field athletes, for the sport was new to the country – less than five years old. Footraces at Sunday school picnics or field days held at schools and on public holidays, such as Dominion Day and Queen Victoria's birthday, provided occasions for schoolgirls to compete. Once they finished their education, however, athletic opportunities were limited and never taken seriously. Events for the "gentler sex" at track-and-field meets were offered as a break in the routine rather than as part of the regular program. Without encouragement and chances for serious competition, young women reluctantly gave up their athletic dreams and confined their running to softball diamonds and basketball courts.

All of this changed in 1923. Needing a promotional gimmick for the Canadian National Exhibition's Athletic Day, the Ex's sports director decided to put girls' events on the program. The emergence of outstanding Toronto athletes at the competition and the resulting publicity encouraged many to take up sprinting. Soon athletic clubs for women in Toronto were arranging meets and providing an affiliation for those interested in track and field. The progress of the sport was remarkable. By 1928, girls' athletics had advanced to such a degree that Canada's first female contenders at an Olympic Games were considered favorites in four of the five events.

The six chosen to represent the country knew their ability and believed they would do well. Yet they never saw themselves as pioneers preparing the way for future female Olympians. Nor was their reason for going motivated by any heroic ideal. They went abroad for the purpose of winning for Canada, the team manager said, and that goal came before everything else. One of the team's members, Ethel Smith, also recognized this. "We just felt that they took us over to run and it didn't make any difference if we were the first women or not," she said. "We were there to compete and win. That was the main thing."

This is their story. It's one of joy and disappointment, an opportunity lost, and an act of extraordinary sportsmanship. It contains heroes and a villain, who, ironically, was a Canadian. Above all, it's a tale about a small group of women athletes who became known as the "Matchless Six," and what they did at an Olympiad long ago.

Chapter Two

The Olympic Games –
Reserved for Men

A t the first modern Olympics in Athens, there were no elaborate opening ceremonies, no march-past of athletes from different countries, no lighting of the Olympic flame. Instead, on the mild and cloudy afternoon of April 6, 1896, King George I of Greece, surrounded by members of the royal family, stood in the royal box of the reconstructed Panathenaic Stadium and declared the Games opened. This was followed by cannon salvos, the release of pigeons, and a massed choir singing a cantata composed for the occasion by a Greek musician. An enthusiastic crowd of 40,000 looked on, and thousands more, who couldn't afford the admission price, packed the surrounding hills.

Large numbers of women were present, eager to witness the revival of the Olympic Games. At the ancient Games, they had been banned both as spectators and competitors. Any woman caught was liable to execution; flung to her death from a cliff called the Typaean Mountain. Fortunately, it never happened. The only recorded offender, a woman called Kallipateira, was pardoned when it was discovered her father and three brothers were Olympic champions and her son had just won an Olympic victory.

At the first modern Olympiad, women were still excluded from participating, but not from attending. And while they were welcomed, their parasols weren't. Organizers felt the umbrellas would inhibit the view of others in the stadium. Despite this prohibition, women weren't discouraged from attending the Games. For ten days, they were enthusiastic supporters, watching and applauding as the contestants vied for Olympic titles. American athletes dominated the track-and-field program, winning nine of the twelve events, but a Greek was victorious in the contest that mattered most to his countrymen — the marathon.

Among those present in the stadium the first day was a thirty-two-year-old French nobleman. A tiny man, only 5 feet 3 inches tall, he sat near the royal box with the other dignitaries. A large bushy mustache dominated his face, giving him the appearance of a terrier, and dark brown eyes, crowned by thick eyebrows, conveyed a sense of authority. Baron Pierre de Coubertin, a convert to the idea of resurrecting the Olympics, had dreamed of this moment for the past four years. He first suggested it in 1892, at a meeting of

Baron Pierre de Coubertin, founder of the modern Olympics, watched over the Games like a protective parent. Throughout his life, he opposed women's participation in the Olympics.

IOC/Olympic Museum Collections

French sportsmen. Although the idea met with applause, approval, and good wishes, no one fully grasped his vision. Some inquired amusingly whether women would be allowed to attend the new Games as spectators. Others asked if the athletes would compete in the nude in order to prevent the weaker sex from watching the competitions.

Still de Coubertin persisted and, in Paris two years later, he convened an athletic congress attended by 2,000 delegates representing thirteen countries. He made such a powerful appeal, the delegates voted in favor of reviving the Olympic Games in Athens in 1896. When the government of Greece refused to support them, the Greek public rallied to the cause and raised the necessary funds. The Games were an outstanding success and Greeks everywhere felt a sense of national pride. For de Coubertin, the revival of the Olympics marked the beginning of a lifelong commitment to the Olympic movement.

Following the Athens Olympiad, he became president of the International Olympic Committee (IOC), a group of men that had the authority on all questions concerning the Olympics. In the beginning, the committee was the baron's creation. He chose the fourteen members, gentlemen amateurs drawn from the upper classes. The majority were almost exclusively absent, allowing him a free hand in Olympic matters. He was also the committee's sole means of financial support, which further strengthened his control. Clearly in charge, de Coubertin used his position, his numerous writings, and *La Revue Olympique,* the committee's monthly newsletter, to promote his ideas. The subject of women was among his favorite topics.

A product of the Victorian age, de Coubertin reflected its values and attitudes. For him, woman's role was to be man's companion and mother of the family. As such, sport was outside the "feminine sphere" and the weaker sex who participated in physical activities violated "the laws of nature." In so doing, they put their health at risk. But more alarming, these female amazons, lacking maidenly shame, would never find husbands. If women wished to participate in sport, de Coubertin argued, they should do so from the sidelines, cheering their husbands or helping in the sport education of their sons. At the 1912 Stockholm Olympics, he singled out a Swedish

Author's collection

The appearance of women on the slopes of Switzerland riding downhill on sleds upset de Coubertin as being ugly and indecent, especially the awkward position they had to assume.

woman whose six sons were taking part in the Games. The IOC awarded her an Olympic medal for being true to the ancient ideals.

De Coubertin held a dim view of the modern sports crowd, believing they were like small children who needed to be taught how to behave. Not surprisingly, he was deeply disturbed by the thought of young women competing in front of such company. "The sport spectator must always be watched morally," he warned. "One must know what he is looking for and why he is there." It wasn't a problem for the male competitor, as the crowd was there for the sport, yet it was different for the females. They attracted the type of spectator who came not for the game, but to leer at the participants. This was dangerous, he contended, as the spectacle of lightly clad, sweating women engaged in strenuous activity would have an unsettling moral effect on the men who watched.

Given de Coubertin's feelings about women and the Olympic Games, it was ironic that female contestants first appeared at an Olympiad in his native country. Held as part of a World's Fair, the 1900 Paris Olympics were judged a disaster. De Coubertin and the Olympic organizing committee, hopeful of repeating the success in Athens, were pushed aside by those in charge of the fair. Sports were relegated to a secondary role, displaced by exhibits of French industrial technology. Nowhere was the word "Olympic" to be seen and the Games were referred to as the "Paris Championships," or the "Great Exhibition meeting."

The sports events, which lasted between May and November, were reduced to sideshow attractions. Ice-skating, for example, was grouped with the cutlery display; sailing was part of the life-saving exhibits. But included among the contests were two events for women – golf and lawn tennis. One of the nineteen women who competed was Charlotte "Chattie" Cooper of Great Britain. Described as "a quite unusually strong and active girl who scarcely knew what it was like to be tired," Cooper won the women's singles tennis event and became the first female Olympic champion. The winner of the ladies' golf event, Margaret Abbott of the United States, was the second. Abbott had a decided advantage when the French competitors misunderstood the nature of the game and turned up to play in high heels and tight skirts.

Although de Coubertin confessed it was a miracle the Olympic movement survived Paris, the Games were precedent setting for women. From two events, their program expanded over the next four Olympiads to include archery, fencing, figure skating, swimming, and diving. Still, their numbers remained small, comprising less than two percent of all those competing. At the 1924 Paris Olympics, they exceeded one hundred for the first time. Yet the 136 women represented only four percent of the total.

The feminine presence sometimes produced situations unusual for the Olympic Games. At the first postwar Olympics, held in Antwerp in 1920, American figure skater Theresa Weld provoked a minor flap when the judges cautioned her for making jumps "unsuitable for a lady." Whenever she leapt into the air, her skirt flew up, revealing her knees. Despite this, she won the bronze medal. An eleven-year-old Norwegian ice-skater caught the fancy of many at the Chamonix Winter Olympics in 1924. During her free-skating routine, the little "ice fairy" stopped frequently to visit the sidelines and ask her coach for instructions. She finished last, but Sonja Henie would win the next three Olympics and become one of the most famous figure skaters of all times. At the 1924 Games, to protect their teenaged swimmers and divers from the evils of Paris, the United States Olympic Committee housed the young women so far from the city that a trip of five to six hours was required to get them to and from the swimming pool. American Gertrude Ederle won bronze medals in the 100 and 400 meters freestyle events, and a gold in the 4 x 100 meters freestyle relay. Two years later, "Trudie" Ederle would become the first woman to swim the English Channel, in a time two hours faster than the men's record.

Although the admission of women to successive Olympiads was contrary to de Coubertin's wishes, the organizing committees weren't ignorant of popular opinions. The events opened to women were those considered aesthetically appealing and likely to display the female body in a positive manner. As sports "of the better kind," they were acceptable to the gentlemen amateurs sitting on the committees. Moreover, they were held in front of small audiences of good character.

Athletics, however, were different. To perform them properly, women had "to breathe heavily, look messy, and sweat." Furthermore, the contests would occur in a stadium full of spectators, many of whom were there to stare at the female contestants. This wouldn't do, and, in 1914, delegates at the Olympic Congress in Paris rejected a resolution to allow women to compete in the athletic category at the next Olympics. Seven Olympiads would take place before female athletes competed in an Olympic arena.

These distinctions mattered little to de Coubertin. For him, any participation by women at the Olympics was illegal. Following the 1912 Stockholm

Olympics, in which female swimmers and divers first competed, he declared that the door must be opened or shut to women. "Can one consent to giving access to 'all' Olympic events to women? No?" he asked. "Then why allow them some while forbidding them others?" For him the answer was obvious – women must be barred from the Olympic Games altogether. But it was too late. Women had already participated and it was impossible to shut them out.

In 1925, de Coubertin resigned as president of the IOC. Poor health and his belief that it was unacceptable to monopolize the presidency caused him to step down. His resignation marked the passing of an era in Olympic history: It also removed a powerful adversary to women's participation in the Games. Hopes were raised that more events would be opened to them. A year later, the International Amateur Athletic Federation (IAAF), the world body responsible for track and field, informed the IOC that it would vote on athletic events for women at the 1928 Olympic Games.

Since its founding in 1912, the IAAF had consistently opposed track-and-field events for women at the Olympics. But a Frenchwoman, Alice Milliat, was determined to change this attitude and worked tirelessly to affect it. Born in 1884, she was well educated and fluent in several languages, earning her living as a translator. She married, but within a short time was widowed. She never remarried, instead committing herself to the advancement of women's sports, especially track and field, and to the admission of women to athletic events in the Olympic Games. It proved a hard battle.

Her initial request for women's track-and-field events at the 1920 Antwerp Olympics was refused by the IOC and the IAAF. Disappointed with their response but not discouraged, she set about to form an international association that would provide opportunities for female athletes. In 1921, the *Fédération Sportive Féminine Internationale* was born. Under Milliat's leadership, it planned, organized, and held the first women's Olympic Games in Paris a year later. Eleven events were on the program and athletes from five nations competed in front of 20,000 spectators. A sports magazine reported that the men present were only interested in the naked legs and thighs of the competitors. Other accounts were impressed with how fast those legs and thighs could go, and how high and far they could jump.

Despite the success of the first women's Olympics and the growing popularity of women's track and field, the IOC and the IAAF were unbending. When Milliat sought athletic events for women at the 1924 Paris Games, they again turned her down. A second women's Olympics were held at Gothenburg, Sweden, in 1926. After the IOC objected to her use of "Olympic," Milliat changed the name to the Second International Ladies' Games. They were another success, the number of participating nations increasing from five to eight.

By now, the men of the IAAF realized their sport and organization were in trouble. A rival association in charge of women's athletics had emerged to challenge them as track and field's only governing body. Moreover, the split along gender lines showed no signs of healing. Something had to be done to insure the future of the sport. In April 1926, a meeting took place between the two sides at which an accord was reached. Milliat and her federation agreed to abide by the rules of the IAAF, effectively placing themselves under the IAAF's control. In return, the women were promised five athletic events at the 1928 Olympic Games in Amsterdam — 100 meters, 800 meters, 4 x 100 meters relay, running high jump, and the discus throw.

On August 5 and 6, the congress of the IAAF met at The Hague in Holland to vote on the agreement. President J.S. Edstrom warned the delegates that they had before them a question of the greatest importance and if the congress voted against women's admission to the Olympics, it meant the division within the sport would continue.

Despite the warning, there was opposition. The Finnish delegate spoke "with vigor" against athletics for women. They were contrary to the classic Olympic idea, he argued. If women were allowed to compete, the Olympics might suffer some measure of ridicule. In addition, athletic sports represented a struggle in which endurance played a great part – something men inherited and women did not. Yet the German representative, who was a doctor, said that medical studies showed that athletic sports were beneficial to women's health and athletics for women at the Olympics would confirm this.

It was the proposal of the Swedish representative, however, that caught the fancy of a number of delegates. He felt it would be fair to give the women a chance of showing what they could do, if only as an experiment, and proposed this for the 1928 Olympic Games. He added that in no way did it commit the IAAF to future Olympiads. But the British delegate disagreed. He felt it would be difficult to dismiss these events from subsequent Olympics if they were accepted in Amsterdam.

Still, the Swedish idea won over many at the congress who saw women's admission to the Olympics as a way of bringing the two sides together. In seconding the proposal, France's representative declared a sporting organization bearing the name "International Federation" had no right to ignore women, one-half of the population. The Dutch delegate, who supported the admission of women's athletics to the Games, was reluctant to see his country's Olympics as the test for the experiment. He suggested unsuccessfully that the inaugural program for women's track and field be introduced at the tenth Olympiad in Los Angeles in 1932. By a vote of 12 to 5, five athletic events for women were added to the program of the Amsterdam Olympics.

In Canada, the IAAF's decision was noted briefly in the newspapers, and five months passed before the question of sending a Canadian women's team to the Olympics was raised. In January 1927, the GIRLS' SPORTS column in the Toronto *Evening Telegram* advised girls of Olympic caliber to drop all other forms of sport and confine themselves to athletics. Now was the time for preparation, it said. Four months later, the Canadian Olympic Committee (COC) announced it would finance "a small but thoroughly capable team of women athletes" for the Amsterdam Olympics. The squad would be chosen by the country's Women's Amateur Athletic Federation (WAAF), subject to approval of the COC. Not more than six girls would go: Four would be sprinters and would also comprise a relay team, one girl would act as a spare, and the sixth would be a high jumper.

It wasn't until November that the WAAF officially decided to send a girls' team to the Olympic Games. Delegates at the annual convention agreed that it would be selected by a committee of the federation working in conjunction with the COC. Besides candidates for the 100 meters, 4 x 100 meters relay, high jump, and discus, the women's federation agreed to send a competitor for the 800 meters, provided someone suitable was discovered. The national Olympic Trials would take place in Halifax in July, in combination with the Canadian Women's Track-and-Field Championships.

It was fortunate for the women that the president of the COC at the time was Patrick Joseph Mulqueen. A popular and influential member of the

Patrick Joseph Mulqueen,
a strong supporter of amateur
sport and female involvement,
served as president of the
Canadian Olympic Committee
from 1922 to 1946.

Canadian Olympic Committee

Amateur Athletic Union of Canada, the men's body responsible for amateur sport, the sixty-one-year-old Mulqueen had been in charge of the COC since 1922. The job proved challenging, but his testy and confrontational personality was well suited to deal with the organization's problems, especially that of choosing a Canadian Olympic Team every four years. He was never one to work quietly behind the scenes to resolve a wrong. And whenever an unfairness occurred, he pulled no punches in demanding justice. An Irish temper coupled with a short fuse didn't help, and he was always ready "to 'explode' on the spot." Yet his reputation for generosity, kindness, and selflessness was well known. Athletes who traveled overseas found him always ready to help. He frequently provided money out of his own pocket and sometimes bought track shoes for those in need.

Pat Mulqueen, or P.J. to his many friends, was a strong supporter and advocate of women's sports from their earliest days. He was especially active in girls' track and field. It was because of him and Dr. A.S. Lamb that Canadian female athletes had been invited to participate at Stamford Bridge, London, England, in 1925. When an athletic meet was needed to choose the team, he helped organize it. He served as a member of the selection committee that picked the squad, and his efforts in raising money allowed the athletes to travel to England first-class and to have proper uniforms and equipment. Upon their return, they were warmly received by a reception committee in Toronto, headed by P.J.

He welcomed the admission of women to athletic events in the Olympic Games. For he knew that Canada, particularly Toronto, boasted athletes of world-class ability who would do well internationally. Now that the opportunity had arrived, Mulqueen was committed to sending a team. Those chosen, however, wouldn't be the first of their sex to represent Canada at an Olympic Games. That distinction belonged to Cecil Eustace Smith, a fifteen-year-old figure skater from Toronto who participated at the inaugural Winter Olympics in Chamonix, France, in 1924. Yet the team selected for Amsterdam would be the first to compete at a Summer Olympics and the first to compete in athletics.

The decision of the COC to send women athletes to an Olympic Games wasn't acclaimed. They would be "excess baggage," some said, a "feminine millstone" around the neck of the Canadian Olympic Team. Others argued that the Olympics, old and new, had operated well on the principle of no female participation. Why change now? But the Toronto *Globe* disagreed, saying that it was absurd to compare the state of women in ancient Greece with that of modern women. Today, in every field and calling of life, women were playing a grand part, the *Globe* contended, and there was no reason why they shouldn't exhibit their prowess on the athletic field.

The debate didn't end with the selection of Canada's first women's team, but continued into the Olympics and beyond. For many, female involvement in the Olympic Games was another troubling example of the changes occurring in postwar Canada. Women already possessed the vote; they smoked and applied makeup in public; they went everywhere unchaperoned. Where would it end?

Canadian Olympic Committee

A "fancy skater" from Toronto, fifteen-year-old Cecil Eustace Smith was popular with the British press, much like the Canadian women's Olympic team four years later.

Chapter Three

Sport Was Their Life

The backgrounds of the six who comprised Canada's first Olympic women's team weren't unusual. Two were high-school students, two were office secretaries, one was a factory worker, and one was a business college student. They lived at a time in Canada that was called the Golden Age of Women's Sport. Everywhere, unprecedented numbers of young women played softball and basketball; bowled on alleys and greens; rowed, curled, swam, sprinted, and speed skated. "Women were getting bored and needed to expand their energy," a sportswoman of the time explained. "Games looked interesting and exciting. They did not want to grow up like their mothers, who were taught to be ladylike, and learn to take care of the home. They wanted to prove they could do things men could do."

As women embraced a more active lifestyle throughout that golden decade of the 1920s, they showed that sport was no longer solely a male activity. "Canadian women were not just knocking at the door of the world of sport," one male observer remarked, "but had crashed the gate, swarmed the field, and in some cases, driven mere men to the sidelines." World champions in speed skating, basketball, and sprinting emerged to emphasize the

This cartoon, published in the *Toronto Sunday World* in 1924, depicts the extent to which many young Canadian women were playing competitive sports.

Myrtle Cook Scrapbook

point. In all of this, the members of Canada's first women's Olympic team were no different.

Myrtle Cook's career as a competitive track athlete wasn't long – only eight years. She entered the sport older than most and, for the first half of her athletic career, she ran in the shadow of another. Still, she never abandoned her goal of being the best and pushed herself until she achieved it. "The greater the ambition, the greater must be your determination to give up pleasure to one controlling purpose," she said. "Make every move up a winning one."

Myrtle Alice Cook was born in Toronto on January 5, 1902, the first of two children to Alfred and Jenny Cook. She was a shy and introspective child, yet her relationship with her parents was close. Alfred Cook, who worked as a securities carrier for Wood Gundy, was an important influence and often provided advice in times of crisis. Her mother was also supportive, particularly of her daughter's athletic efforts. Before each competition, Jenny Cook would tuck a note of good luck in one of Myrtle's track shoes.

Myrtle began school at Earl Grey Public, where her love of physical activities took root. She played basketball, but excelled at running. First-place ribbons from the school's Annual Games in 1913, 1914, and 1916 are pinned in her scrapbook. Schoolmates who raced against her realized they would "have to run some to beat Myrtle." She attended Riverdale High School, where she gained further renown as a sprinter by winning the Toronto Interscholastic 100 yards Championship. After graduating, she became a legal secretary. As a working woman, athlete, and later, coach, her days were full.

Typical of her generation, Myrtle participated in more than one sport. A proximity to Lake Ontario led to an interest in canoeing. Ironically, she couldn't swim and was petrified of the water. Nevertheless, when the Kew Beach Canoe Club was formed, she joined the Kaybee Girl Paddlers, a group of young women eager to learn the sport of war canoe paddling. She was a member of the Beaches Amateur Athletic Association ladies' hockey team the year it was runner-up for the city championship in the intermediate section. She also played interchurch basketball, bowled five pins, and subsequently took up speed skating, golf, and tennis.

While these activities provided Myrtle with exercise and competition, it was sprinting that opened her eyes to the further benefits of sport: travel,

City of Toronto Archives, Fonds 1244 Item 158

Despite the handicap of bulky skirts and petticoats, these young women did their best to run fast in this footrace on Toronto Island, *circa* 1907.

Author's collection

The numbers bowling five pins grew substantially after World War I. Myrtle Cook belonged to one of the first bowling leagues organized for women in Toronto and the popularity of the sport increased when long dresses were replaced with shorter styles.

recognition, and fame. "What can be sweeter than the million dollar feeling a girl gets when she steps off a train at some strange town knowing that her advent has been heralded by posters on telegraph poles, in store windows, and on billboards," she said. Yet, as one of fourteen members in a war canoe or ten on a hockey team, individual recognition was difficult.

Sprinting was different, Myrtle realized. It was a sport you won on your own merit – no stick, ball, bat, or anything to help out, just your own feet and your prayer that they moved quickly. She always enjoyed running and winning races at school meets, but after graduating from high school, she discovered that occasions for competitive sprinting ended. Like many of her fellow athletes, she reluctantly gave up the sport.

In the summer of 1923, an unforeseen opportunity arose. Women were invited to compete for the first time at the Canadian National Exhibition's Athletic Day, the country's premier track-and-field meet. Seizing the chance, Myrtle set in motion an athletic career that would lead to international honor and acclaim.

In the twenties, young women who played a number of sports, and played them well, were called all-rounders. It was a celebrated title that very few earned. Within this select group, however, there was one who stood head and shoulders above the rest. Fanny Rosenfeld, who excelled in track and field, hockey, basketball, and softball, was the complete sportswoman. A reporter claimed that she was possibly the most proficient all-round sportswoman in the world.

Born in Dneipropetrovsk, Russia, on December 28, 1904, Fanny was the second of five children of Max and Sonia Rosenfeld. She was better known as Bobbie, a nickname she acquired as a teenager when she was the first girl in the family to have her hair cut short, or "bobbed." A month after her birth, Bobbie, her older brother, and her parents fled the country because of religious persecution and anti-Jewish pogroms. They immigrated to Barrie, Ontario, where relatives were already living. In time, Max established a successful used-goods business on Collier Street, opposite Trinity Anglican Church. Bobbie attended Central Public School and Barrie Collegiate Institute, where she established a reputation as a fine athlete. In this, her father was her biggest fan. Her mother, however, thought games too strenuous and rough, and didn't share her husband's enthusiasm.

According to family history, the first race Bobbie ran and won occurred at a picnic in Barrie. She and her sister Gert arrived to discover they had lost their lunch money. Learning that one race had box lunches as prizes, they entered. Bobbie was leading at the end of the race. Just before she crossed the finish line, she reached back and pulled Gert over the line after her, and they had their lunches.

As Bobbie got older, her renown as a runner spread throughout the area. But it was the Great War Veterans Association track meet at the Barrie Fairgrounds in August 1922 that fixed her reputation. Confident in her ability, Bobbie issued a challenge to any woman to meet her in a race of 100 yards. Her speed was well known and no one stepped forward, so she dared the boys. When several agreed to take her on, she was given a three-yard advantage and beat them easily. She was so proud of the trophy she won, her first, that she refused to allow the local jewelers to do the engraving, but took it back to Toronto instead.

A few months earlier, the Rosenfelds had left Barrie and moved to the Queen City. For Bobbie, it was the best thing that could have happened. Women's sports were booming in Toronto and opportunities to play organized basketball, hockey, and softball were plentiful. She joined a basketball team in the YWCA Industrial League. At the same time, she competed in the ladies' section of the Toronto Hockey League, which was just beginning. Her play at center for North Toronto stood out, and the *Toronto Daily Star* reported that her skating, stickhandling, and shooting were equal to that of most boys in the junior hockey league. "I liked hockey best," she said. "I liked the speed of it. It enthralled me." That summer she played softball at Sunnyside in the Major Ladies' Softball League, the city's first softball league for women. Her ability and intensity marked her as someone to watch.

Author's collection

By the 1920s, the long, cumber-some skirts first worn by women hockey players had given way to shorter outfits, allowing greater freedom and speed.

A year later, in 1923, her softball squad was in Beaverton, Ontario, for an exhibition game against another Toronto girls' team, as part of a sports meet. Afterwards, the players were invited to compete in a 100 yards race. Bobbie was persuaded by team members to enter and, in spite of her baggy bloomers, rubber-soled shoes, and crouch start, she won, defeating the Toronto city champion, Rosa Grosse. Within a month, Bobbie would race again. This time it would be in front of 15,000 people screaming her name as she charged down the track.

Ethel Smith grew up knowing economic hardship. Her father was fre-quently out of work following the war, and times were hard. Clothes were often hand-me-downs or made over. Because education was a luxury for the struggling family, Ethel quit school after grade eight and, at fourteen, went to work for Superior Embroidery in Toronto's garment district. Sports became an outlet. When her long day on the factory floor was done, she would take the streetcar home, where her mother would have supper waiting. Afterwards Ethel would put on her "big fat bloomers" and set off for a game of softball or basketball.

Ethel May Smith was born in Toronto on September 24, 1907, the second youngest of Michael and Eliza Smith's eight children. Despite privations, Ethel and her siblings grew up in a home that was loving and supportive. Her father encouraged his children to take part in any sport that came their way, and would often play catch with them or watch their games. The bespectacled Smith needed little coaxing because she enjoyed sports. At field days in public school, she competed in the high jump and the running broad jump, but was especially good at sprinting. In her senior year at Norway Public, she was a member of the volleyball team that won the city of Toronto title.

Ethel's love of sports continued after leaving school and she played basketball with St. John's in the Interchurch League and softball in the Beaches Girls' Senior League. During the summer, she would travel to Sunnyside to watch some of Toronto's best women ballplayers. There were no bleachers then, only a rope encircling the field that marked the area where spectators could stand.

On the Civic Holiday in 1924, Ethel won a footrace for women at a field day sponsored by the Beaches Businessmen's Association. This seemingly insignificant event marked the beginning of an athletic journey that would take her to the pinnacle of the sport four years later.

The first thing one noticed about Ethel Catherwood were her striking good looks. These were complemented by her height: At 5 feet 10½ inches, she was noticeable. When Toronto sportswriter Lou Marsh first saw her, he declared that she seemed more like a Charleston partner for the Prince of

Wales, the future king, than she did an athlete. "One glance at Miss Ethel Catherwood, the star from Saskatoon," he declared, "and the boys will think they are attending one of the beauty contests." At a time when girls who played sports were often described as "muscle molls," or "Amazon athletes," her attractiveness set her apart and stirred the public's fascination.

At first, Ethel ignored the popular obsession with her beauty. The wish to be a champion high jumper blazed within her and she focused on that goal. Yet it came too easily. Endowed with a fine athletic ability, she was one of those rare all-rounders who excelled at whatever sport she attempted. Early on, she discovered there was no one to challenge her. Without serious rivals, she lacked the incentive to train diligently. Bobbie Rosenfeld, an astute judge of athletic character, observed something else about Ethel: She could be temperamental. "If she set her mind on any task, she was very likely to accomplish it," Bobbie said. "But if her enthusiasm turned cold – she likely would abandon the idea entirely." The supremacy Catherwood held in her sport lasted as long as her desire to compete: Once that was gone, her athletic prowess suffered.

Ethel Hannah Catherwood was born in Hannah, North Dakota, on April 28, 1908, while her mother was staying with family to await the birth of her sixth child. Her parents, Joseph and Ethel, had immigrated with their children to the Canadian West in 1906 to work a homestead three miles east of Scott, Saskatchewan. In 1909, Joe Catherwood decided to forsake farming and became a real estate broker. He built an office in Scott and, the following year, moved his family into town.

Ethel grew up an average student, but an excellent athlete. Her father, who was a fine sportsman in his day, encouraged his family to take part in games and physical activities. A friend of the family remembered that Joe Catherwood always roused his nine children to do a little better than the last time. Gradually they developed into a group of athletes that could run faster and jump farther than any in the area.

The Catherwood backyard became a gathering place for the neighborhood children and it was here that Ethel acquired her love of jumping. A high-jump pit had been constructed, where she spent her time practising. She was nine or ten when her father recognized an ability and decided to take her in hand. Under his watchful eye, and with his encouragement, she steadily improved. At fifteen, she could jump 4 feet 2 inches. A year later, he offered her a prize if she could do 5 feet in one week's time. She did it easily. Believing she could do better, he offered a greater prize for a height of 5 feet 4 inches. A week later, she amazed him by jumping it and then doing it again to prove she had mastered it. Unknown to them both, she had leapt higher in her backyard than any woman in the world.

In August 1925, Joe Catherwood moved his wife and four youngest children to Saskatoon. The town of Scott was declining and he felt the province's second largest city offered better economic and educational prospects for his children still at home. The change proved to be a turning point in Ethel's life. Leaving behind the simple existence of Scott, she became part of a growing, bustling metropolis, which was the center of the West's railway network and called the Hub City. She arrived an unknown, one of thousands who were leaving the province's towns and moving to Saskatoon and Regina. Yet, a year later, she would be celebrated throughout Saskatchewan, her name reverberating as far east as Montreal.

At an early age, Jane Bell knew she could run. Her success in races at Sunday school picnics and at playground and public school meets revealed a natural ability that made her a winner. Coupled with this was an intense competitive drive to succeed that belied the devil-may-care attitude she exhibited throughout her life. "I never, ever, give up," she said. "That's the difference between a loser and a winner — losers give up; winners never do." She thrived on challenges, whether it was running at track meets, playing games with her friends after school, or competing in sports. She tried to be the best at everything she did.

Her competitiveness and extroverted personality were reminiscent of Bobbie Rosenfeld. Like Bobbie, Jane was an all-rounder, proficient in track, basketball, softball, and swimming. Despite their age difference, the characteristics they had in common fostered a mutual respect. For Jane, it was closer to hero worship. She thought Bobbie was "a fabulous person" and so much fun to be with. These feelings never changed and, when Bobbie died, Jane felt that part of her had gone too.

Born in Toronto on June 2, 1910, Florence Isabel was the middle child of Ethel and John Bell. Her mother, who was a nurse, named her for Florence Nightingale. But the significance was lost on the active and rambunctious youngster, who thought the name sissy and hated it. Because she was always tripping over things and her leggings were continually falling down, her father started calling her Jane, after "Calamity Jane," an American frontierswoman noted for her shooting, riding, and wild behavior. Soon family and friends picked up the habit, and the name stuck.

Jane's father, a manufacturer's agent for the Wilson Tobacco Company, had played lacrosse in his youth and maintained an interest in sports when his competitive days were over. Because of him, Jane acquired a love of games and physical activities. He would take her skating in High Park in the winter and to baseball games at Hanlan's Point in the summer. When she was ten, he died suddenly from a stroke, removing an important influence from her life. Plans for her to attend boarding school were abandoned, the home was sold, and the family moved to a smaller residence.

Despite these changes, Jane remained a free spirit who was always on the go. Sunday school picnics, bird-watching in High Park, and Girl Guides kept her busy. She and Dot O'Neill, her best friend, would practise high-jumping in Dot's backyard at six o'clock in the morning, or jog around the block. It was at Keele Street Playground during the summers, however, that Jane's love of sports was nurtured. Besides games and crafts, Keele Street held field day competitions with other city playgrounds. Jane discovered she was a natural who could run fast and win. She welcomed the opportunities to test herself against others. An expanding physical education program at Keele Street Public School provided another avenue for her competitiveness, but she always desired more. In the summer of 1923, she was given the chance to race against the best women runners from the United States. She would be one of the youngest participating, but thirteen-year-old Jane Bell was undaunted.

Looking back, Jean Thompson's achievements were almost unbelievable. With less than a year's training in the 800 meters, an event that was regarded as too strenuous for women, the young high-school student from a small rural town in Ontario achieved close to world-record times. Those who knew her weren't surprised. A schoolmate recalled that Jean was a shy quiet girl who had only one thing in mind, and that was to be the best at what she wanted to be. She began as a sprinter and high jumper, but her coach realized that her prospects in these events were limited and turned to the middle distance race of 800 meters. Within a few months, he took the seventeen-year-old, who had never run farther than 100 yards, and turned her into one of the country's best prospects for a medal at an Olympic Games.

Jean was born in Toronto on October 10, 1910, the fifth of seven children to David and Margaret Thompson. She lived for a time in Hamilton before moving to Penetang, Ontario, where her father began work for the Dominion Stove Company as a molder. Growing up in the small community, Jean was an active child who enjoyed the outdoors. In the summer she played softball, earning a reputation as the best pitcher in Penetang. She belonged to the Girl Guides, was an active member of the local Presbyterian Church's Young People's Society, and taught Sunday school. Full of fun, she was liked by everyone.

On Labor Day weekend, 1924, her happy life suffered a tragic turn. Her mother was killed in an automobile accident. It was a cruel loss, but Jean and her family dealt with their grief and carried on. A year later, she entered Penetang High School, where she met Lucien A. Wendling, the school's football and athletic coach. A former track athlete, he recognized in Jean an ability and drive to achieve great things. Sparking her interest in track and

Author's collection

The CNE's Athletic Day was held on this track in front of the grandstand. A crowd of 15,000 was present on September 8, 1923, to watch women compete for the first time.

field, he set out to make her the best she could be. Over the next three years, his role would be central to transforming the inexperienced teenager into a world-class athlete.

The numbers attending the final day of the Canadian National Exhibition (CNE) on September 8, 1923, were larger than usual. A second Children's Day had been declared and exhibitors were giving away additional free samples. For sports fans, the attraction was Athletic Day, featuring female athletes that would be competing for the first time in the history of the fair. Ninety girls entered, and many were curious to see how they would do. There was an international flavor to the meet as the sports director of the CNE had invited the coach of four girl sprinters, the "Chicago Flyers," to bring his athletes to compete. Despite a downpour at noon, 15,000 spectators filled the Ex's grandstand.

The Canadian relay team that faced the "Chicago Flyers" at the Ex's Athletic Day in 1923: (left to right) Bobbie Rosenfeld, Myrtle Cook, Grace Conacher, and Rosa Grosse. Cook described their costumes as "the strangest outfits ever to hit the speedways."

Doreen Stokes

Four heats were scheduled in the 100 yards open race for girls, with the first two finishers in each heat qualifying for the final. If marks were given for attire, the young women from Chicago were clearly the winners. "There they were," Bobbie Rosenfeld said, "prancing up and down the track, attired in eye-fetching short shorts and clinging jerseys . . . and spike shoes yet. And here we were looking like yokels in our blue serge bloomers, blousie middies . . . and running shoes yet." Before the meet, Bobbie had hunted in vain all over town for something to wear. She ended up dressed in her brother's swimming trunks, her father's socks, and the white top of her Hinde and Dauch softball uniform. "I must have looked hideous," she said.

The performances of the local girls, however, were at odds with their comical appearance. Facing a strong wind, and running on a sodden track,

Canada's Sports Hall of Fame

Myrtle Cook Scrapbook

The exciting finish of the 100 yards final for girls at the Ex's Athletic Day, won by Bobbie Rosenfeld (in white), and close behind, Rosa Grosse (in black).

The success of the Canadians at the Ex's Athletic Day gave athletes like Bobbie Rosenfeld increased exposure in the newspapers, as this cartoon from the *Toronto Sunday World* shows (note the misspelling of her names and the wrong birthplace).

Bobbie Rosenfeld and Rosa Grosse won their heats, each only a fifth of a second over the world's record. Myrtle Cook was runner-up to Rosa and qualified for the final, as did another Canadian, Grace Conacher. Lost in Rosa and Myrtle's heat was a thirteen-year-old representing City Playgrounds: Jane Bell gave it her best, but the older runners were too strong. She wasn't discouraged. The experience only whetted her appetite. She would be back.

The 100 yards final was exciting, and the crowd was on its feet cheering as Bobbie overcame Rosa's early lead and won by six inches. The American champion, Helen Filkey, was third, three yards behind, and Grace Conacher and Myrtle Cook were fourth and fifth. The thrilling finish and the results of the race left the fans delighted. The two Toronto girls, despite their inexperience and need of proper sprinting apparel, had beaten the well-trained Americans.

The relay team's victory was just as remarkable. Rosa, Grace, Myrtle, and Bobbie, ignorant of relay running fundamentals, and never having competed together before, finished first. City reporters, who weren't expecting much from the local runners, were exultant. "WHEN CANADIAN GIRL SPRINTERS TRIUMPH," blazoned one headline; another announced, "TORONTO GIRL ATHLETES WIN. BEAT BEST FROM CHICAGO."

The Ex's Athletic Day was a breakthrough for women's sprinting. Because it was the first time female track athletes had appeared at such an important meet, they received unprecedented publicity. The surprising victories of the Canadians were especially significant in raising the sport to a new level. Previously, running contests for women had consisted of egg-and-spoon races, needle-threading races, and three-legged races at picnics and fairs. From now on they would occupy a larger stage, involving competitors from other countries vying for world records.

There were some, however, who regarded the rise of women's sprinting with the same foreboding as they did hockey, softball, and basketball. Doctors, teachers, and clergymen asserted that games and strenuous physical activity belonged to "men's sphere," and women who participated would be

Women's egg-and-spoon races were popular at picnics and fairs before World War I. Here a group of women charge forward, while attempting to balance an egg in a spoon on Toronto's Centre Island in 1909.

"unsexed," or masculinized. They would lose their feminine charm, the traditionalists fretted, and their roles as future wives and mothers would suffer. The troubling signs were already apparent in the mannish clothes, the flat figure, and the boyish haircut prevalent among the younger generation. More serious, vigorous physical activity would have a detrimental effect on a woman's childbearing capacity. Doctors warned of potential harm to the reproductive organs by running and jumping. Moderation was the watchword, as overindulgence could lead to serious physical and mental effects.

But once girls began playing sports, there was no turning back. Arguments used to dissuade them from games and activities proved fruitless. "The idea of harming ourselves never entered our heads," one young woman said. "We used to get a medical from the doctor, principally covering heart and lungs. That was all. We knew ourselves and knew what we could do." As competitive sports opened up for them, women who worked in business and industry, particularly in Ontario, flocked to courts, rinks, and diamonds.

Sprinting was no different. Those who competed at the Ex's Athletic Day, or read about it in the newspapers, were attracted to the sport. In Toronto, Myrtle Cook, Bobbie Rosenfeld, Jane Bell, and, one year later, Ethel Smith were training and competing to become the best. In Penetang and Saskatoon, Jean Thompson and Ethel Catherwood would also catch the competitive spirit. Over the next five years, the progress of these six Canadian athletes would be remarkable.

The fear that women who took up manly sports would be masculinized was a common one, as shown in this comic postcard from the turn of the century.

THE ATHLETIC LASS

Oh, the girl who goes in for brawn,
Who's in training from daylight till dawn,
    Should from such stunts refrain
    And develop her brain,
And thank us for " putting her on!"

Author's collection

Chapter Four

Becoming the Best

The Athletic Day achievements of the Canadian women, well covered by the newspapers, led to invitations to participate at American indoor meets during the winter. Before then, however, someone was needed to teach the athletes how to run properly. It was important they do well because, from now on, whenever they competed, the women would be linked with Toronto and its Canadian National Exhibition.

Prior to Athletic Day, Walter R. Knox had furnished rudimentary coaching for a couple of the girls. He was asked to take charge of the team and he agreed. They were lucky to obtain his services because no other man in Canada had his general experience in athletics. In his day, he was the best all-around track-and-field man of his size in the world and he'd competed throughout Europe and America. Known to be egotistical and independent, he was prepared to go anywhere to meet the best in their own backyard. His early life had been that of a vagabond athlete, traveling from town to town, making wagers with the locals, and competing against their hometown champions. He rarely lost.

Beginning in October 1923, Knox met with Myrtle, Rosa, Bobbie, and Grace at the Mutual Street Arena – the only facility available. Over the next three months, three times a week, they trained on the arena's broad

A former world-class athlete, Walter Knox was recognized as an authority on track and field, coaching the Canadian teams at the 1912 and 1920 Olympic Games.

Photographs of the Toronto relay team appeared in newspapers and on sports cards in boxes of chocolates and cigarette packs. From left to right: Grace Conacher, Bobbie Rosenfeld, Myrtle Cook, and Rosa Grosse.

The Millrose Games are held annually at Madison Square Garden in New York City. Athletes from the United States, Canada, and Europe, who had turned in record or near-record performances, were invited to compete.

promenade behind the top row of seats. Under Knox's coaching, the girls developed the skills of sprinting and running the relay. They became a common sight to the rink staff as they circled the makeshift track; the sounds of their running shoes slapping the concrete floor and their breath condensing in the cold air.

Indoor competitions followed in early 1924. The girls appeared at the renowned Millrose Games in New York's Madison Square Garden in January. Rosa won the 50 yards sprint, but the relay team came a disappointing third when Grace fell after she was accidentally tripped by another runner. At the Canadian National Exhibition's Athletic Day in September, Rosa continued her excellent running. She beat Bobbie by three yards to win the 100 yards sprint. The relay squad was victorious once more, defeating four runners from Chicago, and setting a world's record.

Myrtle Cook, whose interest in athletics had been rekindled by recent competitions, was hopeful an organization like Toronto's Kew Beach Canoe Club would emerge to encourage female athletes and provide a place to train. Girls playing softball, basketball, and hockey already enjoyed the benefits of coaches, teams, and leagues throughout the city. Those keen on track athletics, however, did not. The lack of experienced instructors, and the absence of an association to look after the sport, meant that female sprinters were on their own. They could depend on their fathers for coaching; train themselves; or quit. Young women like Myrtle Cook, who found these options unsatisfactory, now turned to the Toronto Ladies' Basketball Club, an organization that boasted many of the city's outstanding sportswomen. Rosa and Grace, Myrtle's teammates, already belonged. So, early in 1924, she joined the organization, which became the Toronto Ladies' Athletic Club later that year to reflect its expanding number of sports teams and increasing membership.

Myrtle's connection with the club was never an easy one. Faced with joining a group that had been together for three years, and friends much

Shown here in her backyard displaying her trophies and medals, Myrtle Cook dons the black-and-orange outfit of the Toronto Ladies' Athletic Club.

Don McGowan

longer, she found it difficult to fit in. "We didn't get close to her," a club member said. "She may have had some close friends, but if she did I wasn't really aware of it." As someone who "didn't seem part of the Toronto Ladies'," Myrtle remained on the fringe, associated with the organization but never a part of it. After a year and a half, she left with no regrets.

Her reputation as a sprinter, however, continued to grow. In 1925, she was chosen for a team to participate at an international women's athletic meet at Stamford Bridge, London, England. The competition against athletes from England and Czechoslovakia was the first of its kind for the Canadians. Unfortunately, their inexperience with the javelin and discus and the novelty of international competition proved insurmountable handicaps. The ten athletes failed to win a single contest and the Canadian squad finished last overall. For Myrtle, a third in the 100 yards dash and a second

Josie Dyment (left) and Myrtle Cook (right) take their marks for the final of the 100 yards dash at Varsity Stadium, Toronto, July 11, 1925. The race was part of a meet to select the team to compete at Stamford Bridge, London, England.

on the relay team was the best she could do. It was disappointing, but the experience strengthened her determination to excel in her sport.

Over the next two years, she worked hard to reach this goal, and by the summer of 1927 had made it. Former champion Rosa Grosse, the "Queen of the Cinder Path," was no longer running. Her marriage the year before and the recent birth of a son were now the priorities in her life. Moreover, a congenital inner ear problem, making it difficult for her to hear the starter's gun, had worsened. Myrtle's other serious rival, Bobbie Rosenfeld, was involved with other sports and hadn't competed in over a year. The departure of two formidable opponents from contention, while regrettable for women's track, opened the way for Myrtle. At the Millrose Games in New York in February 1928, she won the 50 yards dash, matching the American indoor women's record. Her victory in the event that Rosa had dominated for the past four years served notice that a new champion had arrived.

Myrtle was now part of the Canadian Ladies' Athletic Club and was its director of track-and-field athletics. Besides training and competing, she was coaching the club's relay team and junior runners for local competitions. The *Toronto Daily Star* observed that her work measured up to that of the best male coaches. But at the moment, Myrtle wasn't thinking about coaching. Her eyes were fixed on distant shores and the Olympics in Amsterdam. The memory of her first international experience at Stamford Bridge still smarted and she desired another chance to compete overseas. Now that it had arrived, she wasn't about to let the opportunity pass her by. Myrtle was committed to making the women's Olympic team.

She had been practising since early May. At five o'clock each morning, she would jog or hitch a ride on a milk delivery wagon to a secret location, where she would train for an hour before going to work. Sometimes during her early-morning workouts, she was accompanied by Ethel Smith, another whose wish to be an Olympic team member was just as great.

Two years before, in 1926, Ethel had joined the Canadian Ladies' Athletic Club at Myrtle's request. Myrtle needed a runner for the club's relay team and Ethel was attracted by the variety of sports offered by the Canadian Ladies'. It proved to be a good fit, and her addition helped the team become the best in North America. Yet those who knew Ethel weren't surprised. Since 1924, when she won the race on the Civic Holiday, her steady progress as a sprinter was marked as she moved from the Toronto Hydro-Electric Athletic Club to the Beaches Ladies' Athletic Club to the Canadian Ladies'.

"I ran for the pleasure of running," she said, in the beginning. "I never dreamed I was going to go ahead." But go ahead Ethel did. At the Ex's Athletic Day in 1924, she qualified for the final in the 100 yards and finished sixth. One year later, competing in the first Ontario Ladies' Track-and-Field Championships, she won the 100 yards race for girls under 18, and placed

City of Toronto Archives, Fonds 1266, Item 11487

Ever since Ethel Smith joined the Canadian Ladies' Athletic Club to run for the relay team, she showed steady improvement. In June 1928, Lou Marsh wrote, "The sprinter who has made the most advance this spring seems to be Miss Smith."

second in the 60 yards low hurdles and standing broad jump, earning a tie for the intermediate all-round title. At the second Canadian Women's Track-and-Field Championships in 1927, she was the 220 yards sprint champion.

In February 1928, Ethel was chosen to compete at the Millrose Games. A crowd of 12,000 noisy fans at Madison Square Garden watched as she and the other Canadians won the relay, finishing four yards ahead of a picked American squad. Her role on championship relay teams and her emergence as a sprinter of note improved her confidence. For the first time, Ethel thought about the Olympics Games and the likelihood of going. The provincial Olympic Trials were in Toronto in June, and the nationals in Halifax twelve days later. Setting her sights on these competitions, she was fixed on making a strong bid for the Olympic team.

"Ethel trained and trained and trained," her younger sister recalled. Myrtle Cook's aunt lived on the street behind Ethel's house and, whenever Myrtle visited, they arranged to run at five o'clock each morning. "We were neighbors and had a signal," Ethel said. "Whoever was ready first would hang a towel from her window, and then we'd meet in front of that house so we wouldn't wake anyone." Before leaving, she would swallow a mixture of raw egg and wine, believing it was good for stamina. Then she and Myrtle would run for an hour through Kew Gardens, or on the Woodbine Racetrack. Afterwards they would have a cup of coffee at a restaurant, go home, wash up and change, then take the streetcar to work.

Some evenings they were joined by a couple of others at the Canadian National Exhibition track, where Ed Percy of the Central YMCA offered simple instructions. "He just told us how to pump with our arms because some of the girls were not using them properly," Ethel remembered. "Then we would run for a while, come home, have our supper, and go to bed." The unsophisticated regimen seemed to work. By the end of May, she was regarded as a serious contender for a place on the Olympic team. Still, it wouldn't be easy, for there was another who was just as determined to make the squad. As the holder of five Canadian records in track and field, Bobbie Rosenfeld demanded consideration.

Bobbie had just finished a long season of hockey and basketball. In April 1928, her Lakeside Ladies basketball team, the eastern Canadian champions, had traveled to Edmonton, where they were unsuccessful in challenging the famous Grads for the national title. Now that basketball was over, Bobbie announced she would compete in the 100 meters and discus events at the Ontario Olympic Trials in June.

Within two years of winning the girls' 100 yards dash at Athletic Day in 1923, she had emerged as the country's foremost female track-and-field

Bobbie was now competing for the Pats Athletic Club and
working for its sponsor, the Patterson Chocolate Company.
Knowing Bobbie's athletic ability and the publicity she generated,
W.A. Patterson formed a club around her. Here she is posing in
her Pats softball uniform.

athlete. Her rise was so rapid and so dominant that her stature in the sport
overshadowed her considerable reputation in softball, hockey, and basketball.
The rivalry between Bobbie and Rosa Grosse, which emerged during the
period, was legendary, and the 100 yards race became the highlight of the
women's program at Athletic Day. Supporters of both, in the thousands,
flocked to the Ex's grandstand to witness the battle for racing supremacy.

The extent to which Bobbie had made athletics her own occurred at the
inaugural Ontario Ladies' Track-and-Field Championships in 1925. Of the
seven events she entered, she won five – the shot put, discus, running broad
jump, the 100 yards low hurdles, and the 220 yards dash – and was second in
two others – the 100 yards dash and javelin. She also set three Canadian
records. It was an exceptional performance and she was exhausted at the end
of it. "Few men can stand such a program in an afternoon, and certainly
none could equal the winnings," one reporter remarked in amazement.
"Miss Rosenfeld stamps herself as the outstanding athlete in Canadian track

Myrtle Cook Scrapbook

The success of Athletic Day featuring women's events resulted in the addition of other girls' sports to the Exhibition program. The rivalry between Rosa Grosse and Bobbie Rosenfeld in the 100 yards open race became a highlight. Between 1923 and 1926, each won the event twice.

As great as Bobbie's contributions were to the Pats hockey and softball teams, it was her single-handed achievements in track and field that raised the green and white of the Pats Athletic Club above those of other organizations.

and field." One year later, at the first Canadian Women's Track-and-Field Championships, she almost duplicated the feat, placing first in four events and coming third in two others.

As "the most promising all-round track athlete in Canada," it was hoped Bobbie would be one of the leaders who would carry the nation's standard to the forefront in international competition. To do this, she was advised to devote all her time and effort to the sport, forsaking all others. But she loved the excitement of hockey, basketball, and softball too much. She could no more give them up than renounce her religion, and she continued to play. A softball injury kept her out of the second Canadian Women's Track-and-Field Championships and Athletic Day in 1927, disappointing her many fans. That winter, a busy hockey and basketball schedule weakened her commitment to the relay team for the Millrose Games. During the two months of practise, Bobbie was present only once. And when the tryouts were held, she was absent. The excuse given was an injury previously suffered in a basketball match, but it was reported that she played both a hockey and a basketball game the same night. Her interest in athletics was waning.

Bobbie was never one to remain on the sidelines, however. The opportunity to become a member of the first Canadian women's Olympic team was too attractive, as was the chance to travel to Europe and perform at an Olympic Games. The lure of publicity and the glare of the spotlight were also irresistible. Bobbie realized early that track and field was the one sport that "took you more places and [put] you . . . in the public eye more."

In early May, 1928, she was practising under Walter Knox. Sportswriter Phyllis Griffiths remarked that for the first time in Bobbie's long and honorable athletic career, she was getting into hard training. She was a certainty for the Olympic team, Griffiths believed, unless something unforeseen happened. Yet Bobbie hadn't competed in track and field for over a year and would be facing seasoned runners, such as Myrtle Cook and Ethel Smith. Furthermore, Rosa Grosse announced her comeback and that she, too, would try for a place on the Olympic team. To tackle these dangerous rivals, Bobbie would need all the speed and skill she could muster. Lou Marsh was confident she could do it. "Miss Rosenfeld of Toronto should have no real difficulty in making her place," he said, "for she is not only a good sprinter, but she shies a mean discus and she will be needed on the relay team."

As Bobbie trained, a younger athlete worked out nearby. Also coached by Walter Knox and equally intent on going to the Olympics, seventeen-year-old Jane Bell hero-worshipped Rosenfeld and was thrilled to be practising in her company. Yet Jane was no starry-eyed youth beginning an athletic career. Her success as an accomplished track-and-field competitor was well known in Toronto. Fiercely competitive and driven, she was expected to give Bobbie and the others a good fight for a place on the women's Olympic team.

Although her sprinting debut had begun unsuccessfully at the Ex's Athletic Day in 1923, Jane had persisted to become a winner. She joined the Toronto Ladies' Athletic Club in the autumn of 1924, which proved pivotal in her athletic life. Surrounded by accomplished sportswomen, she blossomed, becoming a star on the club's basketball and softball teams. But it was the burgeoning sport of athletics that became a passion. At the first Ontario Ladies' Track-and-Field Championships in 1925, she was the all-round

Jane Bell Doane

Jane Bell, in a typical carefree mood, during a trip to a Girl Guide jamboree in Victoria, B.C., in the summer of 1927.

junior champion, winning the 60 yards low hurdles, placing second in both the 100 yards dash for girls under 16 and girls under 18, and coming third in the running high jump.

The next year, as part of the Toronto Ladies' relay team, she traveled to Philadelphia and competed in the city's Sesquicentennial Games against more than one hundred American athletes from twenty-two states. Jane and the other Toronto girls won the relay event, defeating the formidable squad from the Pasadena Athletic Club, and equaling the world's record. One month later, at the Canadian Women's Track-and-Field Championships, she set national junior records in the 100 yards dash and the 60 yards low hurdles.

Throughout her steady progress, Jane was judged one of the rising young stars and great things were predicted for her. In 1927, the talk among girls' athletics was the Olympic Games in Amsterdam and who would go. As a junior, Jane wasn't mentioned in these discussions. Still, she never considered her age a handicap and was confident in her ability. "You can have anything you want," she said, "if you want it badly enough." She knew the selection for the women's Olympic team was only months away. Sportswriters were already suggesting that hopefuls should be on the track during the fall and training inside during the winter. Jane was ready to make that commitment and whatever sacrifices were necessary for a place on the team.

But she realized these weren't enough: Skilled coaching was also necessary, and the only person who could provide this was Walter Knox.

Because of her involvement with track and field, Jane knew Knox and had been coached by him. She appreciated his exacting standards, his ability to get the best from an athlete, and his refusal to accept anything less. "I thought he was wonderful," she said. "I worshipped him." When he was hired as coach of the Parkdale Ladies' Athletic Club, Jane made up her mind. Ending her three-year association with the Toronto Ladies', she moved to the Parkdale club.

For Jane, training under Knox full-time was a dream come true. He knew how badly she wanted to go to the Olympics and he believed she had the talent to make it happen. He told her that hard work and discipline must come first, however, and if she was conscientious about these, he would see that she got there. That was good enough for Jane, who thought he could answer any prayer. But Knox knew from experience that physical training was only half the battle. The other involved the mental side. He instructed his teenaged athlete that each night, before going to bed, she stand in front of her mirror and say, "Good night, Jane Bell, member of the 1928 Olympic team." It was a psychological ploy to build her confidence. Over the next several months, it became a ritual.

Knox's coaching and Jane's hard work were soon apparent. After three years of trying to make the Toronto relay team, she competed as part of the squad at the Millrose Games in February 1928. The Canadians won for the second year in a row, and equaled the indoor record for the quarter mile. A month later, at a meet in Hamilton, Jane upset Myrtle Cook in the 60 yards dash. By May, Phyllis Griffiths observed that she was coming along "like a house afire," and would make a strong bid for one of the six places on the Olympic team.

As she practised with the Parkdale Ladies', Jane became better acquainted with another member whose place on the team for Amsterdam seemed

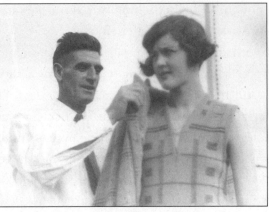

Joe Griffiths, of the University of Saskatchewan, took charge of Ethel Catherwood's training when she moved to Saskatoon. He constructed a jumping pit on a vacant lot at the back of his house and every day he traveled across the city in his Model T Ford to get her.

unquestionable. She had first met Ethel Catherwood at the national championships the previous summer. Unimpressed with both the hoopla surrounding the Saskatoon high jumper at the time and her aloofness, Jane thought her a bit of a snob. Once she got to know Ethel a little, however, she saw a lonely person who missed her family and friends. "I felt sorry for her," Jane said, "because I was with my mother and family. I had a nice home." Their association with Parkdale Ladies' and their Olympic ambitions sparked a friendship that lasted for the next three years. And while Jane and Ethel did all kinds of things together and had their own little jokes, Jane felt she never really knew the girl from Saskatoon.

In 1925, E.W. "Joe" Griffiths, physical director at the University of Saskatchewan, first learned about Ethel when a Saskatoon newspaper reported that she had jumped 5 feet at a local high-school athletic meet. If true, she had set a new Canadian record. Griffiths went to her home, where she showed him she could easily clear 5 feet. Convinced that Ethel would be a world champion if her technique could be improved, he took on the job of training her. A year later, at a provincial athletic meet in Regina, the Saskatoon teenager stunned the crowd when she cleared the bar at 5 feet 2⁷⁄₁₆ inches, an unofficial world's record.

By the summer of 1927, Griffiths realized that nothing more remained for Ethel in the West. She realized it too. "If you are good out there, you are

City of Toronto Archives, Fonds 1244, Item 8179

Ethel Catherwood, as she appeared at the 1927 Canadian Women's Track-and-Field Championships. Her outfit was provided by the Benevolent and Protective Order of Elks, Saskatoon (also known as the Saskatoon Elks Club).

good alone," she said. She needed to face jumpers that could challenge her and motivate her to become her best. The Canadian Women's Track-and-Field Championships in Toronto offered that opportunity. Through Griffiths' efforts and those of a young reporter from the *Saskatoon Phoenix,* the Saskatoon Elks Club was persuaded to cover the costs of sending Ethel and her mother east. The Elks also promised an elaborate track uniform for the Saskatoon high jumper to wear when she competed. One way or another, Ethel Catherwood would make an impression.

More than 3,000 people attended the championships at Varsity Stadium, the largest ever to witness a women's track meet in the city. The publicity given Ethel in Toronto's newspapers prior to the competition was extensive, and many fans were there to see the western athlete in action. They weren't

City of Toronto Archives, Fonds 1244, Item 2117

Lou Marsh had been both a well-known sportsman – accomplished in football, baseball, boxing, and track – and a renowned boxing and ice hockey referee. Starting as an office boy for the *Toronto Daily Star* in 1893, he joined the paper's sports department seven years later and, until his death in 1936, immersed himself in sport and his daily PICK AND SHOVEL column, popular among Toronto sports fans.

disappointed. Clad in a snow-white athletic outfit bearing the crest of the Saskatoon Elks Club, and draped in a purple cape, its collar trimmed in white fur, she was the center of attention. Lou Marsh described the excitement of seeing her jump, and labeled her so uniquely as the Saskatoon Lily that the title endured for the rest of her life. "When Miss Catherwood threw off her long purple cloak with its Elks insignia," he wrote, "and showed herself in her athletic costume of pure white, and the crowd got a glimpse of her symmetrical figure there was a gasp of astonishment, but when she loped quietly up to the bar and 'scissored' her way over 4 feet 6, there was a roar of delight. The crowd knew a high jumper when they saw one and the Saskatoon Lily was one."

A sore leg prevented her from doing better, but Ethel jumped 5 feet ⅛ inch, easily winning the event and setting a new Canadian high-jump mark.

Ethel Catherwood wins the high jump at the 1927 Canadian Championships as the other competitors watch.

Coming onto the field an hour later, she excited the crowd again by tossing the javelin 114 feet 7 inches. It was another Canadian record. An observer remarked that nothing like her form in the two events had ever been seen locally before. With two national records to her name, Ethel was the sensation of the meet. "Never in the history of girls' sports has a visiting queen become so famous in Ontario," the *Regina Morning Leader* remarked.

For those who were there, it was her high-jump victory that was the highlight of the championships. After her record-breaking jump, the lieutenant governor of Ontario walked onto the field and congratulated her. A *Morning Leader* editorial confidently predicted she would be a member of the team that would represent Canada in Amsterdam. The prophecy seemed apt when, less than a month later, she jumped 5 feet 2 inches at the Ex's Athletic Day.

During her stay in Toronto, Ethel met with Teddy Oke, the millionaire sponsor of the Parkdale Ladies' Athletic Club. He promised to send her to Shaw's Business School and provide a secretarial job in his brokerage business if she joined his club. But it was Oke's offer to hire Walter Knox to provide the best instruction in high-jumping that convinced her to leave Saskatoon for Toronto. She had trained briefly under Knox following the Canadian Championships and considered him one of the best. The feeling was mutual. He was keen to coach her because he believed she had the ability to be the world's greatest high jumper.

Ethel returned to Toronto at the end of January 1928 with her sister, Ginevre. Six years older and more outgoing than Ethel, "Ginger" Catherwood was popular and well known in Saskatoon from her University of Saskatchewan days, when her athletic achievements were the talk of the city. She had come east at her parents' behest to look after her younger sister and keep her company. They rented an apartment and began business college. Ethel started training indoors with Knox and was easily jumping 4 feet 10 inches. He expected to have her doing 5 feet 3, or 4, when the warm weather arrived and they were able to practise outdoors. To achieve this, he said, two things were necessary: consistent hard work on his part, and constant and painstaking efforts on hers to follow his instructions.

As Toronto was the center of women's athletics in the country, attention focused on athletes from the Queen City. But, in the past five years, girls' sports had spread beyond Ontario's capital and were growing in communities throughout the province. Accounts of out-of-town athletes occasionally made their way to Toronto. In mid-May, 1928, it was reported that one of them, Jean Thompson of Penetang, had inquired about a twilight meet scheduled for Toronto on June 12. The teenager possessed good possibilities, it was said, and, if she could arrange to stay over until the provincial Olympic Trials, she could profit from the training facilities here.

For the past three years, Jean had been working with her coach, L.A. Wendling. "L.A.," or "Windy" as he was affectionately known, had been a fine athlete in university. As a coach, his methods were somewhat unorthodox, but Jean trusted him and did what he said. They were often seen on Church Street in Penetang: Jean running up and down the road; L.A. driving beside her in his automobile and shouting instructions through the car's open window. In spring, he had her out with the men's baseball team, racing around the base paths with the players. But much of their training took place on the racetrack of J.T. Payette, a wealthy Penetang businessman. L.A. would measure off 100 yards and Jean would practise the distance on the substitute track. To provide competition, he sometimes ran against her himself, or recruited a few of the local boys and girls.

After Jean became unbeatable in the region, her coach looked further afield. The 1927 Canadian Women's Track-and-Field Championships provided a good opportunity to test his student against the best athletes in the country. It was also a chance to gauge her Olympic chances. Although her third-place finishes in the 100 yards dash and high jump were impressive for a sixteen-year-old, L.A. realized she was no match for the Toronto sprinters

Barbara Howard

This photograph of Jean Thompson, taken outside her home in Penetang, Ontario, shows the young runner in training. She was coached by L.A. Wendling, one of her high-school teachers, who recognized her enormous potential.

and high jumper Ethel Catherwood. But Jean's situation wasn't hopeless. There was another event on the Olympic program, one that few girls had taken up because of the distance. If he could turn the Penetang teenager into a good 800 meters runner, L.A. was confident a place on the women's Olympic team would be hers.

All during the spring, he taught her pacing, gauging speed and knowing when to break for the finish, all necessary to win the half-mile race. Because Payette's racetrack was the exact distance and shape of an 800 meters track, they spent much of their time there. As the weeks passed, L.A.'s instructions and Jean's work had their effect. How well she learned became apparent when J.T. Payette and other horsemen, adept in the use of stopwatches, timed her. To everyone's astonishment, she was close to the world's record. Her coach realized he could do no more. Jean was ready for the provincial Olympic Trials.

★

A heavy rain the morning of the Ontario Olympic Trials and overhanging clouds left the track sodden and heavy. The gloomy and threatening weather discouraged attendance and only 1,800 watched the competition. The results in the high jump and discus were expected. Despite the wet ground that made the takeoff difficult, Ethel Catherwood cleared the bar at 5 feet, winning the competition without removing her sweat suit. In the discus, Bobbie Rosenfeld set a new Canadian record with a toss of 108 feet 3¾ inches. The 100 meters provided a couple of shocks when Rosa Grosse and Jane Bell failed to qualify. The time away from sprinting affected Rosa and an attack of nerves affected Jane. In the final, Myrtle was first in 12⅗ seconds, followed by Ethel Smith, Bobbie Rosenfeld, and Jean Thompson. For Jean, a fourth-place finish wasn't the result she desired, but she still had the 800 meters.

The eight runners in the half-mile race began strongly. Yet the pace set by Jean was too fast, and the competitors dwindled down to three. Bobbie Rosenfeld, who had entered the contest at the last moment, was determined to give the Penetang teenager a battle and stayed with her until the final stretch. Jean then pulled away, crossing the finish line thirty yards in front. Her time of 2 minutes 26 seconds was creeping closer to the world's mark. Moreover, she seemed unbeatable in the event. But one final test remained. If she could repeat this performance at the national Olympic Trials, a place on the women's Olympic team was assured.

On the day the Ontario contingent of athletes departed for the national Olympic Trials in Halifax, Phyllis Griffiths spoke optimistically about their prospects. She felt that Jean would smash the world's standard for the 800 meters and, if the track was fast and in good shape, Myrtle Cook would do the same in the 100 meters. Ethel would go after a new mark in the high jump, but she needed to do better than 5 feet 3 inches to get it. Bobbie was improving daily in the discus throw and the night before, at a novelty track-and-field meet, she had thrown the discus over three feet farther than her Canadian record. The Ontario girls were shaping up to "sweep the boards," Griffiths said, and it wouldn't surprise her if the Olympic women's team wasn't an all-Ontario one.

Griffiths' intuition proved farsighted. The day after the competition, she remarked that Toronto had every reason to be proud of the wonderful showing made by its girls at the Olympic Trials and Canadian Track-and-Field Championships. The four sprinters chosen for the women's Olympic team were all Queen City athletes: Myrtle Cook, Ethel Smith, Bobbie Rosenfeld, and Jane Bell. Ethel Catherwood, formerly of Saskatoon but now of Toronto, was the premier high jumper, and Bobbie Rosenfeld was the champion in the discus. Only Jean Thompson, winner of the 800 meters, was from out of town. All were jubilant over their success, but were anxious to get home as they had to shop and pack for the Olympics.

On the evening of July 4, 1928, the train carrying the newly chosen Canadian women's Olympic team arrived at Toronto's Union Station from Halifax. Only a few friends and relatives were there to meet it. The absence of an official or semiofficial civic reception was disappointing, particularly as five of the six team members lived in Toronto. But the lack of any acknowledgment was overshadowed by the joy of their achievements in Halifax.

Prior to the trials, some feared a Canadian women's team would be an embarrassment at the Olympics. Instead, the squad seemed poised to accomplish great things. The women sensed this, and were convinced they would receive their due in good time. Alexandrine Gibb, the manager of the girls' team, admitted as much. The band business was simply postponed, she said, until their return from Amsterdam. Then the town and city hall would have to recognize them.

Others shared this confidence. Phyllis Griffiths professed that it looked as if Canada's women would bring back more laurels than the men had done in past years. Another sports observer was equally assured. "These young ladies . . . should bring honors to Canada in the games at Holland," he declared.

Chapter Five

"A Nice but Foreign Land"

Despite a cool and overcast day, the mood among the 500 well-wishers who invaded the platform of Toronto's Union Station on July 10, 1928, was festive. They were there to bid farewell to Canada's first group of athletes departing for Amsterdam, the site of the ninth Olympiad of the modern era. Consisting of track-and-field athletes, wrestlers, rowers, and swimmers, the squad was on its way to Montreal, where it would board the SS *Albertic* for departure early the next day. The boxers, cyclists, and lacrosse team would follow one week later on the *Empress of Scotland*.

The large crowd was unexpected: The sight heartened Canada's team of female athletes, which was making the Olympic trip for the first time. Gathered at the back of the train, they gladly acknowledged the cheery farewells of relatives and friends, posed for the photographers, and bantered with those on the platform. Words of advice shouted by the happy assembly were answered in kind by the girls. "Now, George, don't smoke too much while I'm away. You know you promised," one of them called out.

Teddy Oke was there to offer best wishes to his Parkdale club's three members that were part of the Olympic squad – Ethel Catherwood, Jane Bell, and swimmer Dorothy Prior. He was paying Prior's way to the Olympic Games to compete in the 200 meters breast stroke. Ginger Catherwood was

Just before the train carrying the Canadian women's Olympic team pulls out of Toronto's Union Station, the girls wave to the crowd of well-wishers. Standing on the train's platform (left to right) are Myrtle Cook, Jean Thompson (hidden from view), Ethel Smith, Ginger Catherwood (Ethel's sister), Jane Bell, Ethel Catherwood, Bobbie Rosenfeld, Marie Parkes, and Dorothy Prior.

also being sent by Oke as company for Ethel. In addition, he had donated six hundred dollars for the personal expenses of the women's team. The Women's Amateur Athletic Federation decided the money would be used for the group's traveling, hotel, and miscellaneous costs, instead of giving it to the girls to spend on themselves. This way the amateur laws would be strictly observed.

At 2:30, the whistle sounded and the train pulled out of the station. The girls remained on the observation platform, waving at the crowd until it disappeared from sight. Entering the coach, they joined the boys' team, which had boarded at Hamilton. Included among the male athletes were some that raised hopes that Canada's results at these Olympics would exceed those of the previous one. At Paris in 1924, not a single medal was won in track and field —

During the 1920s, Melville Marks "Bobby" Robinson was a tireless advocate of sports, especially athletics in Canada. He helped found the Hamilton Olympic Club and was responsible for the 1928 men's national track-and-field Olympic Trials being held in that city.

Edna Robinson

the first time since Canada began participating in 1904. Ted Reeve said their achievements were so dismal that he felt the athletes had disappeared down a manhole. Admitting that previous Olympic teams had embarked in "fear and trembling," Lou Marsh declared that this year's team was different. It was "loaded to the nines" with confidence, he said, and good things were expected. One reason for this assuredness was Percy Williams, a twenty-year-old sprinter from Vancouver, who had tied the Olympic record for the 100 meters at the men's Olympic Trials in Hamilton. His coach wasn't surprised, and predicted Williams would win the event in Amsterdam.

The officials chosen by the Canadian Olympic Committee to take charge of the men's track-and-field team – Captain J.R. Cornelius, coach; Robert "Bobby" Kerr, captain; and M.M. "Bobby" Robinson, manager – were all Hamiltonians. Although Melville Marks "Bobby" Robinson was a small man, he stood tall in Hamilton as one of the city's foremost sports enthusiasts and editor of the *Hamilton Spectator*. His choice as manager was deemed an able one. The team would be in good hands with Bobby Robinson looking after its affairs, it was said. Aggressive and fearless, Robinson would play no favorites, and would keep everybody on their toes.

It didn't take long for him to crack down. When the train stopped at Trenton, he called a special meeting of the women's squad and laid down the law concerning diet and other matters. At an athletic competition in Hamilton the previous Saturday, he had noticed some of them drinking pop. They couldn't win on pop, he told them. From now on they would be in strict training and would be expected to live up to the schedule, the same as the men. They could enjoy themselves after they won at Amsterdam.

The lecture had a sobering effect and the girls were subdued as they reflected on Robinson's words. Their quiet mood soon passed and a sense of excitement returned. With the exceptions of Myrtle Cook and Bobbie Rosenfeld, none of them had been on an ocean liner, and Bobbie was too young to remember. The spontaneous farewell ceremony at Union Station delighted them, as did Mayor McBride's promise of a public reception on their return, no matter what happened at the Olympics. An unshakeable self-confidence also boosted their spirits. Manager Alex Gibb remarked that her charges seemed like a girls' basketball team bound on nothing more serious than a friendly game with a rival school. They were certain of winning at least three world championships and teased the men about who would do better in Amsterdam. There were twenty-nine members on the men's squad entered in fourteen track-and-field events, but the women were sure their team of six competing in only five events would tally more points.

As the person in charge of the girls' team, Alexandrine Gibb was well acquainted with the role. She held a similar position when a group of women athletes competed at Stamford Bridge in 1925. Outgoing, forthright, firm in friendship, argumentative, Alex Gibb was all of these. She had been a good basketball player, and afterwards had a long administrative affiliation with the Ladies' Ontario Basketball Association. Trained as a secretary, she made her reputation promoting and encouraging women's sports through her columns in the *Toronto Sunday World*. Her interest in feminine sport was broad, and "Battling Alex" Gibb never faltered as the champion of sportswomen

Canadian Olympic Committee

Canadian Olympic Committee

Alexandrine Gibb was an early feminist who fought for the rights of women to play and control their sports. In 1928 she was hired by the *Toronto Daily Star* to write a column. IN THE NO MAN'S LAND OF SPORT: NEWS AND VIEWS OF WOMEN'S SPORTING ACTIVITIES became the platform for her opinions.

Agnes Elsie Marie Parkes was prominent in coed sports and athletic organizations at the University of Toronto. A founding member of the Women's Amateur Athletic Federation of Canada, she played an important role in the organization's formative years.

everywhere. An ardent feminist, she fought the inequities between men's and women's sports and crusaded tirelessly for equality. A newspaper article described her as someone whom men were continually brushing against and coming off the worst. Realizing that a national sports organization for women was necessary, Gibb became a founding member of the Women's Amateur Athletic Federation. "GIRLS SPORTS CONTROLLED BY GIRLS" was her philosophy.

The chaperone of the girls' team, A.E. Marie Parkes, attended the University of Toronto, where she was a member of the tennis, swimming, basketball, and ice hockey teams. After graduating, she worked for the university and continued her connection with girls' sports in Toronto. A strong friendship developed between Parkes and Gibb, based on their work with the Women's Amateur Athletic Federation, their commitment to women's sports run by women, and their closeness in age: Gibb was thirty-six and Parkes, thirty-five. Because of her relationship with Gibb and her experience as chaperone with a number of University of Toronto girls' teams, Parkes was seen as ideal for the position of Olympic chaperone. P.J. Mulqueen agreed, stating that her selection and that of Alex Gibb couldn't "be bettered in either direction."

Although the appointments of Gibb and Parkes decided the issue of officials for the women's team, the problem of coaching remained. As in 1925, this responsibility was Alex Gibb's, and once again little consideration was given to her inexperience. But the team, realizing a good instructor was essential in the days ahead, knew Gibb wasn't the person for the job. "We asked the question about coaching," Jane Bell said, "but nobody gave us any answer." The obvious choice was the men's coach, Captain J.R. Cornelius, but as Jane remembered, "Cap Cornelius would have nothing to do with the women's team, coaching or otherwise. He refused to do it. He didn't like women. He really didn't like women." When it appeared they would be on their own, they turned to the captain of the men's track-and-field team, and he agreed to instruct them. "Bobby Kerr was the women's coach," Jane said. "He was the one who trained us, how to pass the baton, and so on. We all just loved him."

The train arrived at Montreal's Bonaventure Station at eleven o'clock in the evening. It was thirty minutes late, but Mayor Houde, a number of men prominent in athletics, and about 100 friends of the team were there, waiting patiently. When the athletes finally appeared, the mayor mounted a truck and

Bobby Kerr was an outstanding sprinter who won the 200 meters race and placed third in the 100 meters race at the 1908 Olympic Games in London. Well known in Hamilton for his work in athletics, he helped organize and administer the training camp for Olympic hopefuls prior to the 1928 trials.

Canadian Olympic Committee

welcomed them, wished them luck, and expressed the hope they would bring back many honors. In response, the young women and men gave His Worship and Montreal a round of cheers. The impromptu show concluded, they gathered up their luggage and boarded buses for the ride to the White Star liner *Albertic*. Fatigued from the day's events, they went straight to bed. And when the ship sailed at four o'clock in the morning, they were sound asleep.

The next day they awoke to the *Albertic* steaming down the St. Lawrence towards Quebec City. Because of the late hour at which the Olympic teams got settled away, Robinson, Cornelius, and Gibb decided to give the athletes a break and forego training. The ship arrived at Quebec City at 1:30 in the afternoon. As it docked, the SS *Shawnee* from New York, tied to the same pier, broke into gala attire, with many flags flying in honor of the Olympic party.

At five o'clock, the *Albertic* cast off and the Canadian Olympic Team settled in for a week's ocean voyage before they docked in England. At dinner, Coach Cornelius informed the boys' team that dancing was forbidden until after the Olympics. This created a fine argument, especially as a number of American schoolgirls were in tourist class, on their way to Europe to spend the summer sightseeing. The men were particularly peeved because the women's team was permitted to dance until ten o'clock. In justifying her decision, Alex Gibb said that it was unwise to keep sixteen-, seventeen-, and eighteen-year-old high-spirited girls under too close a system of training.

After dinner, Pete Walter of the men's team and Jane Bell, hearing the music and seeing passengers dancing on the deck below, said, "Why not?" If the no-dancing rule for men was enforced on the first class deck, then they would go down and have "a little swing" on the tourist deck. After enjoying themselves, they returned by the back steps, just in time to see Alex Gibb and Marie Parkes making their rounds. Quickly dropping to their hands and knees, the two wayward athletes crawled under the lifeboats to avoid detection. Bell reached her cabin, quickly removed her clothes, and was in bed in time for the curfew check.

Believing their ruse had worked, and feeling smug about it, Jane and Pete discovered otherwise the next morning. The officials gathered both teams on deck and, without naming names, laid down the law and reminded everyone about the rules. The athletes were told that anyone disobeying commands would be sent home as soon as the ship docked in England. The lecture achieved its purpose. "I was a little bit scared," Jane admitted. "It didn't happen again."

To accommodate the needs of the fifty-two athletes on board, the White Star Line had built a special gymnasium for the wrestlers, rowers, and athletes. A canvas pool was also constructed for the swimmers, who had ropes attached to their waists to keep them from breaking through the sides when they used it. During the ocean voyage, the girls observed a regular training schedule under the direction of Bobby Kerr: physical exercises on the upper deck at 7:30 each morning, followed by a brisk walk; a saltwater bath around 8:00; breakfast at 9:00; a workout in the gym around 10:30; play until noon; luncheon at 1:00; a three-mile walk from 2:30 to 3:30; deck games; dinner at 6:00; dancing in the evening; bed at 10:00; and a visit from the chaperone and manager at 10:30 to insure that everyone was in bed and the lights were out. Each evening, before they turned in, the girls were serenaded by the boys, who stood out in the rotunda and sang, "Good Night Ladies."

As their training was easy, the women had time to relax and enjoy life aboard ship. For Jane Bell, whose big adventure until now had been a railway trip to Victoria with her Girl Guide troop, the voyage made an impression. The experience of traveling first-class, a stewardess drawing her bath each day, dressing for dinner each night, ordering off specially printed menus, and being served by waiters in the dining room affected the teenager. "We were in the lap of luxury," she said. "I thought this was something. I thought this was heaven." The magnificence of sunrises and sunsets on the open sea and the occasional glimpses of whales, icebergs, and porpoises opened her eyes to a larger world.

Like Jane, Jean Thompson had never traveled far from home. Because she came from a small town, she was called farmer by the others. In Amsterdam, when the girls encountered the old-fashioned crank telephone, they kidded Thompson. "Come on, farmer," they said, "you'll know how to work this." Jean accepted the nickname in good humor, preferring it to the Penetang Pansy, which she hated. The other girls thought it awful too. As the youngest on the team, Jean was always regarded as the baby and was never prominent. "She was not a leader by any means," Jane said. "She was fun, but didn't confide in anybody. She didn't tell her secrets." Still, Jane liked her and the two became friends.

If Jean Thompson was withdrawn and shy, Bobbie Rosenfeld was brash and outspoken. She was acknowledged as the comedy queen of the Olympic party, with her antics and funny sayings. One morning, when the seas were rough and only the brave ventured out for breakfast, Rosenfeld advised the girls to drink plenty of milk. It didn't scratch coming up, she said. As the *Albertic* passed through a field of icebergs off Belle Isle, she took one look and exclaimed, "I feel right at home. Look at all the Izebergs." Passing on bridge and chess as too intellectual, she joined a penny ante poker game with the boys, where her comments kept the players and spectators in stitches. Much to everyone's disappointment, this was Bobbie's first and last card game. The women's chaperone, Marie Parkes, put an end to it.

Rosenfeld's fondness for practical jokes also kept the ship's party in a continual roar. On one occasion, sprinters Johnny Fitzpatrick and Percy Williams were the targets of her hijinks. They shared a table in the ship's dining room with some of the women's team. Every night at dinner, a dish of bonbons decorated the table. Williams and Fitzpatrick always arrived first and cleaned the dish before anyone else could get near it. Deciding to teach the boys a lesson, Bobbie persuaded the dining room steward to replace the bonbons with decorated mothballs. On the opening note of the dinner gong, Williams and Fitzpatrick arrived at the table in record time and lunged for the candies. "You should have seen their faces at the first crunch," Rosenfeld gleefully recounted. As much as she loved jokes, Bobbie was never hurtful. She cared about how others felt, but, as Jane observed, "She didn't care what people said about her."

In a close vote, the members of the girls' team elected Myrtle captain over Bobbie. Alex Gibb felt it was a wise choice as Myrtle had "the necessary experience and ability to handle the job." Her association with the squad that went overseas in 1925 and her role as athletic director for the Canadian Ladies' A.C. recommended her for the position. As captain, she worked with Bobby Kerr to insure everything ran smoothly. Kerr was showing the sprinters how to use the relay baton given them by the Hamilton Olympic Club. It was much larger than what they were accustomed to, but the baton was regulation size and they needed to get used to it. Myrtle, with her tiny hand, found it was like lugging a baseball bat.

★

They arrived at Southampton on July 19. Awake at dawn, they were soon busy looking after their baggage, hauling it past customs and onto the tiny toylike train for London. The treatment of the girls by the customs officials, however, proved an unhappy introduction to the Old Country. Gibb complained that some of the officers didn't seem to grasp that they were dealing with a set of athletes and not a troop of showgirls. The officials insisted on digging right down to the bottom of some of the bags. A few words of welcome from the mayoress of Southampton, and the Canadians were on their way.

At Stamford Bridge they had a light workout and were surrounded by movie cameramen, photographers, and reporters anxious to know more about the young women whose record-breaking feats had been circulated abroad. Another reason for the media interest was the absence of an English women's team at the Olympics. Unhappy with the limited program of five athletic events, they had decided to boycott the Games.

The journey by steamer from Harwich to the Hook of Holland was noisy and cramped. The crush of tourists traveling to the Olympics forced the girls to share two small second-class cabins on a vessel whose steering gear seemed bent on coming right up through the hold. It was like trying to sleep in a boiler factory, Lou Marsh reported, and Bobbie joked that, during the trip, she had the best and shortest sleep of her life. Arriving in Holland at five o'clock in the morning, the tired Canadians happily discovered the Dutch customs officers were more obliging. They asked only one question – "Olympic?" – and allowed the athletes to pass, no baggage opened, and board another dinky little train for Amsterdam.

A weary group of athletes entered the city at nine o'clock and were scattered among four locations. They were given the morning to recover from the frantic pace of the past twenty-four hours. The idea of an Olympic village had been abandoned by the Dutch as too expensive. Unfortunately, this prevented the various nationalities from mingling and becoming acquainted. "We didn't associate with athletes from other countries," Jane said. "We met them on the track." The absence of a village also produced a

A bond developed between the women's and men's Olympic teams in Amsterdam. The boys would visit the girls at their boardinghouse, and friendships, such as those between Ethel Catherwood and Percy Williams, and Myrtle Cook and Vic Pickard, flourished.

scarcity of accommodation in Amsterdam. Teams were forced to find lodgings wherever they could, which meant small hotels, school buildings, and boardinghouses in the city, or further afield in Bloemendaal, Haarlem, Hilversum, and Utrecht. The Americans solved the problem of housing by bringing their living quarters with them. Their ship, the SS *President Roosevelt*, became the team's floating hotel during the Games.

Living quarters for the Canadians had been arranged several months in advance by Dr. A.S. Lamb, president of the Amateur Athletic Union of Canada and manager of the Canadian Olympic Team. He was already in Amsterdam to insure that everything was organized and running smoothly. Despite Lamb's efforts, Lou Marsh judged their hotel accommodation as poor, but the best available. The men's track-and-field team was lodged in the Holland House hotel, directly above a beer hall where a mechanical jazz-band hand organ played until one o'clock in the morning. After a few nights of this, Bobby Kerr and Bobby Robinson would go out every evening at 10:30 and have the police cool the enthusiasm of the Hollanders.

Space was another problem. Each small room was occupied by four athletes, who slept on uncomfortable-looking beds. The forty to fifty occupants were also required to share the hotel's two baths. This was inconvenient enough, but the Canadians soon discovered there was a financial cost involved. The hot-water taps were padlocked and a sum of thirty-five cents Canadian had to be paid to unlock them.

At first the women crabbed about their accommodation. The Pension Regina, located on De Lairessestraat in the suburbs, was a small boarding-house some distance from the men, and the girls felt isolated. The complaining stopped, however, when they learned about the conditions at Holland House. Moreover, they were only five minutes from the practise and Olympic stadiums, away from the noisy city crowds.

Initially, Dutch food was another difficulty. "They made the soups so thick, you couldn't tell what was coming up on the spoon," Myrtle Cook said. "The meats were smothered in unknown sauces and two meat courses were served with every meal." Bobbie Rosenfeld was the only one who could manage the diet. Alex Gibb soon eliminated the soup entirely and insisted on plain beefsteak for luncheon each day during competition week. Once the food problem was solved, the girls settled in. Letters home, buying souvenirs such as lace hats and wooden shoes, training in the practise stadium, and visits from the boys every evening became their routine. Gibb reported they were all happy Canadians in "a nice but foreign land."

Upon their arrival in Amsterdam, the men and women were met by Dr. Lamb, who gave each of them a map and a mimeographed letter containing detailed information about places of interest and how to get around. At first they thought the city strange, with canals running through its center, quaint and narrow streets, and old-fashioned buildings. Jane was impressed by its size

Amsterdam had been trying to get the Olympic Games since 1912, but had lost its bid to rivals. The city withdrew its application for the 1924 Olympics when de Coubertin requested them for Paris to mark the thirtieth anniversary of the Olympic movement. In return, Amsterdam was promised the 1928 Olympics.

and cleanliness. When she saw someone scrubbing the steps of the boarding-house where they lived, she was amazed. Pole-vaulter Vic Pickard was struck by the stench of the canals, which seemed to cling to everything. He complained that the milk and tea tasted like the canals smelled, and even the vegetables were tainted with the odor. Another gripe was the close and humid night air that made sleeping difficult.

Still, there was a familiarity about the place that reminded the team of Canada twenty years ago. The use of bicycles by the city's residents recalled a day when Canadians depended on the two-wheelers as a popular means of travel. In Amsterdam, it seemed everybody owned a bicycle. The narrow streets were full of cyclists, sweeping by in droves. At each stoplight, it was interesting to watch them wait for the signal in groups of hundreds, then mount and speed off with elbows and pedals flying.

Those who lacked the courage to try one of the city's zooming taxis found the quieter pace of the streetcars more to their liking. They were never crowded, and moved slowly enough to permit passengers to jump on or off at any point. At the back end of each car was a red letter box for the convenience of the passengers. At first, the girls were unaware of this and one of them mistakenly dropped a letter in a fire-alarm box. Then they learned that anyone wishing to post a letter could do so by chasing after a streetcar. Myrtle Cook recalled: "We did some merry old sprinting, mailing our letters back home."

Elsewhere, correspondents from English-speaking countries discovered their press tickets were printed in Dutch, German, and French. Any information they received from the Dutch Olympic Committee was unavailable in English. When they requested English translations, they were ignored. The treatment didn't sit well with some, who griped that without the English-speaking countries the Olympic Games would be a flop.

As the media struggled with the problem over language, Bobbie handled it in her own unique fashion. Having decided to hire a hack for a tour of the city, she, Jane, Jean, and Ethel Smith approached a group of drivers. Instead of trying to speak Dutch, Bobbie addressed them in Yiddish. To everyone's surprise, one of them understood. Then, with Bobbie in the driver's seat, whip in hand and driver's silk hat on her head, she steered the horse and carriage through the narrow streets while the others admired the sights. When Bobby Robinson and Vic Pickard needed a taxi to go from the practise stadium, Bobbie told the driver where they wanted to go.

Dutch currency was another difficulty Bobbie solved. Shortly after settling into the Pension Regina, Bobbie, Jane, Myrtle, and Ethel Smith went to a bank to change their Canadian money. Each had ten Canadian dollars they wished converted to Dutch gilders. Bobbie was put in charge. "She came back with all this money," Jane said, "and we didn't know who was to get what. So we put it all in the middle of the floor of the bank's vestibule and we got down on our hands and knees. Then we decided, 'Jane, you take one of these; Myrtle, you take one of these.' It took the longest time, but we had more fun than you can imagine. When we had all exactly the same, there were two coins left over. How could that be? Who was to get them?"

On the afternoon of their arrival, the Canadian women began training at the old Amsterdam stadium. A shortage of practise facilities and the large number of athletes present allowed them only two hours each afternoon. At their first workout, they were watched closely by the U.S. coaches, who seemed especially interested in Jean, Myrtle, and Ethel Catherwood. When the Americans attempted to scout the Canadians by timing the sprinters and measuring the discus and high jump, the women purposely screwed up.

Author's collection

The Olympic Stadium, covering an area of over 40 acres and accommodating 40,000 spectators, was the showpiece of the Olympic facilities. Two years before, the site had been one vast swamp. Designed by Dutch architect Jan Wils, the stadium had been built by driving 4,500 piles, varying in length from 36 to 48 feet, into the soft ground. The surface was then raised six feet by transporting a million cubic yards of sand to the site by barge.

Ethel failed to jump 4 feet 10, Bobbie underthrew the discus by eight feet, and the sprinters ran so slowly that the Americans learned nothing.

Meanwhile, all wasn't well with the Olympic Stadium. After visiting the facility, U.S. officials were appalled by the condition of the track. They found it soft and spongy, wholly inadequate for an Olympic Games. It needed resurfacing, they said, with a mixture of cement and cinders, for a harder covering. The dismayed American head coach declared that only a miracle would have the track in proper shape for the opening of the Games. And when a brief strike by overtaxed laborers working on the Olympic field occurred, it seemed even a miracle wouldn't be enough. For the time being, the Olympic Stadium was declared off-limits. This was unwelcome news to the athletes, who complained they needed to be on the track to test its turns and straightaways in preparation for the races ahead.

The swimmers added their voices to the unhappy chorus. The Americans were upset about the brackish state of the water and a dead fish in their pool. The Australians complained of dirty water. When they discovered a dead dog floating on the surface of theirs, it was the final straw. The tanks were drained and replaced with fresh water. The situation was no better for Dorothy Prior, the lone Canadian female swimmer. After practising in a slimy pool and after much red tape was unraveled, she was allowed to train with the men at the Marine Dock. The only problem was, following each sprint, the swimmers had to loosen their suits and discard their catch of shrimp. The Canadians set a record of sorts by being the first to use the Olympic pool. After it was filled, the boys snuck under the barbed-wire fence that night and swam in it in their underwear.

In the days prior to the Olympic opening, the Canadian women found themselves drawing attention wherever they appeared. On the practise field, they were mobbed by other athletes, newspapermen, and spectators. "The team was very, very popular with the public and the press," Jane said. "Everything we did and everywhere we went, we were followed by somebody.

Canada's Sports Hall of Fame

Ethel Catherwood trained under Alex Gibb's supervision. During practises prior to the Olympics, Catherwood became the most photographed girl on the training field.

They would come up to where we lived. We were besieged for photographs." It became difficult to practise as people pestered them for autographs, or wanted to talk to them. Reporters gushed about "the beautiful Canadian girls." Amused by this, Jane remarked, "It was *not* a good-looking team outside of Ethel Catherwood. The beautiful team was Ethel." When someone thought to ask the beauteous Ethel how high she could jump, she answered, "High enough to win."

As the other teams arrived and began their preparations, the Canadians assessed the competition. They were curious about Kinuye Hitomi, the only woman on the Japanese squad. She had been the sensation of the second Women's Games in Gothenburg, Sweden, two years before, when she won the long jump and the standing broad jump, and was second in the discus and 100 yards dash. Sport observers in Amsterdam stamped her as "the most wonderful all-round contestant" and declared she could even defeat Ethel Catherwood in high-jumping. Myrtle watched her in training as she broke very fast off her mark, beating her male teammates. She would be one to heed.

The Canadians were warned about the German women's track-and-field squad. At nineteen members, they were a large team — only the American squad of twenty-one was larger. But after observing the Germans in practise, Alex Gibb was unimpressed. The French were considered the most dangerous opponents in the sprints as they had been training for six weeks and were adept at beating the gun. Yet, the day the French athletes appeared at the practise stadium, they mobbed Ethel Catherwood at the jumping pit and the sprinters on the track. They thought Ethel was wonderful, and confessed they were afraid of the Canadians, particularly in the sprints and high jump. Even the Australian runner who practised with the girls proved to be no match for the Canadians' speed. Gibb noted that they could spot her five yards in every hundred and still beat her.

While the sprinters practised under Bobby Kerr, and Alex Gibb supervised Ethel Catherwood, Jean Thompson was left to look after herself. "She had her own program," Jane said. "She knew what she was to do and how to run. Nobody coached her." For two days, the plan worked well. But a week before the Olympics began, it all came apart. Jean was jogging on the track when Jack Walter, the 1500 meters runner, came up beside her. Unwilling to let him pass, she accelerated, and soon they were racing each other. It was a fatal mistake. The loose cinders of the track, which gave a spongy effect, threatened the runners with pulled tendons and sore muscles. Jean soon felt a pain in her left leg and stopped completely when it became unbearable. She was taken to the Pension Regina and her leg was massaged. The next day it was still sore and she was told to rest it for three days. Before they left Canada, her coach had warned Canadian officials against her running with the men. For a brief moment his admonition was forgotten and it led to Jean's undoing. She had been a favorite to win the 800 meters. Now it was uncertain.

A few days later, Jane suffered a shin splint, a sharp pain in her shin from running, and joined Jean on the injury list. The soft practise track, which Canadian officials said would have been scorned by most high schools at home, was beginning to affect the runners. After Ethel Catherwood and Dorothy Prior suffered a slight attack of hives, Bobby Robinson remarked in frustration, "It is just one thing after another."

As opening day of the ninth Olympiad approached, Lou Marsh reported the Americans were plainly unpopular. Their display of wealth and power and their desire to obtain privileges denied others were resented by everybody. When 150 American track athletes, accompanied by an army of coaches, trainers, and attendants, arrived at the practise stadium the first day, it was an impressive sight. Yet the big show didn't excite Bobby Robinson, who remarked that the Americans made a noise wherever they went. In fact, American cockiness rankled. Four days before the Olympics began, 17 members of the U.S. girls' swimming team broke training and left for a shopping tour of Paris. When questioned about it, they explained that as no one at the Olympics could beat them, the days lost wouldn't jeopardize their chances. During a visit to the SS *President Roosevelt,* Robinson, Mulqueen, and others were told by the Americans that they had left better sprinters at home than Canada had here. As guests, the Canadians held their tongues and said nothing, but the arrogance was hard to take.

The fine weather that had persisted for the past week and a half broke the day before the opening ceremonies with a torrential rainstorm. That afternoon, during a halt in the downpour, the Canadians practised their march-past for the opening ceremonies. Earl McCready, the big wrestler from Regina, would carry Canada's placard and lead the team into the

Canada's Sports Hall of Fame

Joe Wright Jr. is recognized as the best rower in the world after winning the Diamond Sculls.

stadium. Behind him would follow the standard bearer, Joe Wright Jr. Earlier that month in England, Wright had won the Diamond Sculls, symbolic of international rowing supremacy. He was only the second Canadian to do so. In recognition of his accomplishment, he was given the honor of carrying the flag. The Canadian team officials would come after Wright. The women would be next, given pride of place at the head of the Canadian Olympic Team at the ninth Olympiad. Jane and Jean wouldn't be among them, however, excused from the procession because of their injuries. The effects of marching and standing for three hours on cold ground were too risky. Besides, as Alex Gibb reminded them, they weren't here to take part in a parade but to win their races. They could wear their uniforms and would watch the opening ceremonies from the grandstand.

The eve of the Olympics found a confident Bobby Robinson looking forward to the start of competition, convinced that the Canadians had wonderful chances in all branches of sport. He felt the Canadian girls were the favorites in the 100 meters, 800 meters, the high jump, and the relay. Yet Lou Marsh wasn't as optimistic. The injury to Jean threatened her success in the middle distance race, he said. She hadn't worked out since hurting her leg six days ago, and further rest was recommended. Jane's shin splint endangered her chances in the 100 meters and those of the relay team. Another concern was Myrtle, who was feeling the strain of competition. Bobbie lacked the physique and coaching of her European rivals in the discus and would be lucky to finish sixth. Still Marsh believed Bobbie and Ethel Smith were good prospects in the 100 meters if the track was slow. Ethel Catherwood appeared to be the best hope for the team, despite the stout opposition she was expected to face. Those who watched her practise thought she would jump 5 feet 5 inches before she was beaten.

Regardless of Marsh's gloomy predictions, Alex Gibb was satisfied the team would be ready when the competitions began. Admittedly, Myrtle had been nervous, but was settling down and would be alright if the track was fast. Also true, Bobbie would face strong opponents in the discus. Yet her prospects in the sprint were good. Jean would be set for the 800 meters, notwithstanding her sore leg. She still had another four days before the 800 meters trials. Although Jane's chances in the 100 meters were doubtful because of her shin splint, she would have almost a week's rest before the relay.

Among the women themselves, the feeling of self-assurance they brought to Amsterdam remained undiminished. "We didn't care about the United States, Germany, or whoever," Bell said. "We were the best and we were convinced that we were going to win." The news that they were all drawn in different heats for the first round of the 100 meters trials in forty-eight hours augured well. Alex Gibb was convinced that two, perhaps three, Canadians would be in the finals. "The girls' condition is not nearly so tense as that of the men," she said, "and I am confident we will be somewhere in front in spite of the injuries that have befallen the team."

Chapter Six

A Good Beginning

The weather for the opening ceremonies of the ninth Olympiad of the modern era wasn't promising. The series of thunderstorms that had swept into Amsterdam the day before threatened to last not only hours but days. Shortly before the Olympic pageantry began, however, the skies half-cleared and the rain stopped. Yet Lou Marsh was apprehensive, as he sat among the world's press in their section of the stadium. Would the Canadian team be overlooked in the reception given to the immense squads from the United States, Germany, Poland, and Holland? Would Canada's athletes receive scattered applause and be downhearted or discouraged by the mighty cheers expected for the Americans, Germans, and others?

At 1:45 P.M., the Dutch consort, Prince Henry, arrived and was received by members of the IOC and the Dutch Olympic Committee. The monarch, Queen Wilhelmina, would have normally welcomed the athletes, but a religious controversy over holding competitions on Sunday had arisen and she stayed away. As the dignitaries arrived in the Olympic Stadium, the Royal Military and Marine Bands struck up the Dutch national anthem, and a massed chorus of 1,200 choristers from singing societies throughout the Netherlands joined in song. Immediately following the anthem, the march-past of the athletes and officials of the participating nations began.

The Canadian Olympic Team marches smartly into the Olympic Stadium led by Earl McCready, holding the placard announcing "CANADA," and Joe Wright Jr., bearing the Canadian Red Ensign.

For the first time at a modern Olympics, Greece led the parade: The host nation, the Netherlands, was last in the procession. Between them, in alphabetical order by country, according to the Dutch language, came the other teams. Over 5,000 representatives from 46 countries began their circuit of the track, saluted the prince consort in their own national fashion, and lined up facing the royal box. As the fifth nation in line, Canada's entrance into the stadium was announced by Earl McCready, "a giant of a man," bearing the placard "CANADA." He was followed by Joe Wright Jr., holding the Canadian Red Ensign, a wide smile spread across his face. "You could see his white teeth clear across the stadium," Marsh said.

Behind McCready and Wright marched the Canadian athletes, three abreast in rows of 35. The women's team was at the front, their white uniforms, red hats, and red shoes conspicuous. For Bobbie Rosenfeld, the spectacle and thrill of taking part in the Olympic parade were memorable. "You just have no idea how your spine tingles when you march past the royal box at an Olympic Games, in your uniform and behind your standard bearer," she said.

The preceremony jitters quickly disappeared in the thunderous applause that greeted the Canadian Olympic Team. Every now and then a spectator would stand and shout "Canada," to which some members of the group would wave in acknowledgment. As they passed the Dutch choir, cries of "Beautiful Canada" echoed across the enclosure. In front of the saluting stand, the men removed their hats and the entire team, following the dip of the flag, threw out their right hands in the Olympic salute. His earlier doubts dispelled, Lou Marsh declared that Canada was acclaimed, thoroughly, generously, and wholeheartedly. Alex Gibb was surprised by the roar of applause they received.

The U.S. team, 300 strong, was judged smart-looking in black and white, but the effect was spoiled by the girls wearing different colored shoes. In passing the Stand of Honor, the flag bearer refused to dip the Stars and Stripes. Instead of saluting, the Americans merely gave an eyes right. Some felt that at a purely sporting event, they might have followed the same procedure as the other nations. From her place in the competitors' section, Jane Bell thought the parading Americans left much to be desired. "We were not impressed with the United States because they came strolling in, waving to the crowd, while everybody else marched to the music nicely," she remembered. "They didn't lower their flag. And we all said, 'Why didn't they lower their flag?' Now we found out afterwards the United States lowers their flag to no one. But they shouldn't take part in the ceremony if they aren't prepared to show their respect." The crowd in the stadium felt the same. An American reporter described the reception of the U.S. team as "lukewarm."

For Jane and Jean, the disappointment of not marching in the parade was offset by the sights and sounds of Olympic pageantry. They were enthralled by the massive Olympic Stadium, the Olympic flame burning for the first time atop the Marathon Tower; the Olympic flag being raised on the main flagpole; and the release of a thousand pigeons, symbolizing doves of peace. The cheers and applause from the crowd of 40,000, especially when the Canadian team entered the arena, thrilled the two high-school girls, as did the artillery salvos, the crashing bands, and the whirring airplanes.

The Germans, pleased to be part of the Olympics once more, were present in large numbers. Germany and its allies had been excluded from the 1920 and 1924 Olympics as punishment for the war. Now they were back, and the German supporters gave their athletes, "big stolid-looking fellows and sturdy girls in black and white," a warm reception during the march-past. Also, for the first time, loudspeakers allowed everyone to hear the speeches.

All of this was new and exciting for the two Canadian teenagers, who declared the show a "wow." It helped that they were in uniform and had with them some of the boys who were also barred from the opening-day parade because they were competing tomorrow. The only sour note in the festivities was the confiscation of 2,000 cameras, which was done to protect the Olympic photographic monopoly. Dutch detectives, equipped with field glasses, lay on their bellies within the stadium. Scanning the crowd, they were able to spot anyone taking pictures and seize the cameras.

On Monday, July 30th, the weather conditions were windy but otherwise ideal for the opening trials of the 100 meters, which marked the beginning of the women's competition. Thirty-one competitors were entered in nine heats, with the first two finishers in each moving on to the semifinals. Many small flags were evident in the stadium and the crowd of 25,000 was noisy in its support of the athletes. They anticipated with curiosity the sight of women competing in an Olympic arena for the first time. For the correspondent of the French newspaper *Le Figaro,* the spectacle was "the picturesque event of the day." Watching the young women sprint down the straightaway, their bobbed hair flying, he admitted that sports had produced a different feminine figure. Looking like a man with her short hair, the new woman had arrived, he declared, and it was well to get used to her. Yet Baron Pierre de Coubertin never would. In a written message to the athletes and participants at the Amsterdam Olympic Games, the founder of the modern Olympics lamented the admission of women to an increasing number of contests. Still, he predicted the Olympics would survive this, just as they had survived the war.

The Canadians, excited and hopeful of doing well, arrived at the stadium for the 100 meters trials and discovered that no dressing room was provided for them. Manager Alex Gibb put it down to someone's impression that their chances were so poor that they were forgotten. She complained, and was told they could share one with either the Germans, Americans, Czechoslovakians, Poles, or Belgians. Gibb chose the latter. The problem solved, the girls prepared for the task ahead.

Before they left Canada, predictions had been made that they would trim the competition in the Olympic sprints. Some regarded these forecasts as hometown talk, but others believed the results at Halifax proved they were justifiable. The women themselves were confident they would easily reach the semifinals. "They had told us there were supposed to be two qualifiers from every heat," Jane said. "So we didn't think that would be any trouble at all."

Eighteen-year-old Jane was given the distinction of being the first Canadian woman to appear in competition on an Olympic track. Although she had missed four days of valuable training time because of her injury, she was certain she would do well in her trial. "I was excited about it," she said, "but I was pretty sure I would come one or two." The emotion of the moment caused her to beat the gun, and she was charged with a false start. The second attempt to begin the race was successful. Fearing a second false start and disqualification, Jane held back and was behind as the runners got away. At the halfway mark, however, she had overtaken all of them except one. Over the final fifty meters, it was a two-women race as she closed on the front-runner, Kinuye Hitomi of Japan. It was an epic struggle until the finish, with Jane just failing to catch the leader and losing by three yards. Nevertheless, her

National Archives of Canada/PA151007

The first semifinal heat in the women's 100 meters. Bobbie Rosenfeld is first (second from left) and Ethel Smith is second (far left). Both qualify for the final.

second-place finish was "most gratifying" and satisfied everyone. She qualified for the semifinals, but more important, her running showed a return to form, raising hopes for a Canadian victory in the relay.

In her heat, Bobbie started slowly, but quickly made up ground. At the 50 meters mark, she passed the leader, Elizabeth Robinson of the United States, and, over the last thirty meters, coasted home, looking over her shoulder at the finish. Myrtle was hard-pressed by the New Zealand girl, but was able to hold on to win. Ethel won her trial easily. Her time of 12⅗ seconds tied Bobbie's as the fastest in the first round. The results delighted Alex Gibb, who expected at least two Canadians would qualify for the finals.

The semifinals began at 3:45 P.M. Three heats were run, the first two finishers qualifying for the final. In the first trial, Bobbie and Ethel finished one-two, well ahead of the others and with little effort. Although she started well, Myrtle weakened and finished second to the American Elizabeth Robinson, but good enough to qualify. It was left to Jane Bell to provide a clean sweep. "I remember being really excited in the semifinals," she said. "The fact that I was in it." The race began and she got away to an excellent start. "I can remember the ease with which I was running," she remarked. "I just thought that someone was pulling me along. I was winning, and I thought, 'This is so easy.' I saw this string and I put up my arms, thinking I had won. All of a sudden, everybody else went past me." She had mistaken the string from a previous race for that of her own. Pulling up too early, she finished third behind two Germans. It was disappointing and no one was more downhearted than Jane. "When everybody asked me what happened, I explained about the string," she said. "They thought I was making an excuse for not getting into the final."

While Jane's loss was unfortunate, Canadian officials were jubilant that three of the six runners in the final would be wearing the Maple Leaf. Alex Gibb exclaimed they were sitting pretty and could hardly be kept out of first place. Yet the favorite, Myrtle Cook, had run two mediocre races and a Canadian correspondent observed that she was a bundle of nerves. Still, he was optimistic she would find herself and run as she had in Halifax. He called Bobbie to win the 100 meters final, but worried one of the German girls, Helene Schmidt, might "upset the cart." Lou Marsh was hopeful the Canadians would finish one-two-three. He thought Elizabeth Robinson was the only one who had a chance against them.

Bobbie Rosenfeld's results and emergence as a favorite in the sprint final had been a surprise. Prior to the Olympic Trials, she had hurt her knee playing softball and wasn't at her best in Halifax. In Amsterdam, an impressive victory in the first round of the 100 meters, followed by another win in the semifinals, showed an unexpected return to form. Yet Bobbie had been brought to the Olympics for the discus throw, not the 100 meters. Her race results, however, changed everything, and presented Alex Gibb and Bobby Kerr with a big problem. The discus and sprint finals were scheduled for the same afternoon. It was possible for her to do both, as the field event began at 1:00 P.M. and the race at 4:35 P.M. Still, Gibb and Kerr were reluctant to risk it, believing her efforts in the discus might hurt her chances in the sprint. The last word was Bobbie's. After a long consultation with Kerr, she decided to run in the 100 meters and to withdraw from the discus.

Under the circumstances, it was a smart decision. Before the Games, a Polish girl was throwing the discus in practise much farther than anything Bobbie had ever done. This, and the superior physique and style of the Americans and Germans, left many expecting Bobbie would do no better than sixth in the event. A much brighter outcome was anticipated in the 100 meters. Before they left Canada, Myrtle, the world's record holder, was regarded as a favorite to win the event. Yet her disappointing performances in Amsterdam and her nervous temperament were concerns. With Myrtle questionable, Gibb and Kerr knew they needed another to count on. Canada's hopes for victory now rested on Bobbie's shoulders.

Throughout the trials, the running of the Canadians was commended by those who saw it. The correspondent for *Le Figaro* said they were some of the most impressive and best-trained athletes at the Olympics. The reporter for the London *Times* referred to "the fine running of the Canadian girls" in qualifying three of six in the 100 meters final. But it was the reaction of the Dutch fans that was notable. Whenever the Canadians appeared in the stadium, they were enthusiastically cheered by the locals. Each Canadian victory was celebrated as if it were one of their own. In Canada, Mike Rodden, assistant sports editor of the Toronto *Globe,* declared that the high hopes held for the women's team had been confirmed by its results. "There are many who believe that the women athletes of no other country in the world can successfully compete against the 'matchless six' who are wearing Canada's colors at the Olympiad," he said. "The opinion seems justified following the victories scored in the preliminaries."

At 4:00 P.M., the final of the men's 100 meters was held. A small group of Canadians in the competitors' stand endeavored to make as much noise

National Archives of Canada/PA151003

Mike Rodden, assistant sports editor of the Toronto *Globe*, called the Canadian women's Olympic team the "matchless six," and said their victories in the preliminaries bolstered the opinion they were the best in the world. Left to right: Marie Parkes, Bobbie Rosenfeld, Jean Thompson, Ethel Smith, Myrtle Cook, Ethel Catherwood, and Jane Bell.

as they could for Percy Williams, the twenty-year-old from Vancouver and the lone Canadian qualifier. But it was hard going. In one section, 10,000 Germans rose like a great massed choir and cheered when their countryman, George Lammers, entered the stadium. Likewise, the British welcomed Jack London when he appeared. The Americans, not to be outdone, greeted the entry of their champions, Frank Wykoff and Bob McAllister, with similar exuberance. Against such numbers, the Canadians tried their best to encourage Williams. The members of the women's team were waving the Canadian Red Ensign, given them by P.J. Mulqueen. Bobbie Rosenfeld had appointed herself head cheerleader and was leading the Canadian contingent with the chant, "Yea Canada! Yea Canada! Yea Canada! C-A-N-A-D-A. CANADA!"

Down on the track, standing between London and Lammers, Williams looked like a David amid two Goliaths. As the runners took their marks, the

Edna Robinson

The Canadians in the competitors' section of the stadium cheer Percy Williams' victory in the 100 meters.

stadium fell silent. Only the clacking from the typewriters in the press section could be heard. After two false starts, the race was finally begun. The small coterie of Canadians followed Williams' progress up the track, all the while screaming and yelling. At the halfway mark, he appeared to be in the lead. At 70 meters, they were sure of it. Only thirty meters to go, and the athletes flew towards the finish. As they crossed the line, it was the red Maple Leaf that was in front, smashing the tape before the others. Percy Williams had won and the Canadians were jubilant. Grabbing the flag, Bobbie waved it to and fro and tried to start an organized cheer, but everybody was too excited to follow along. They just roared until they were hoarse. Percy's victory had carried them "up into a seventh heaven of joy."

From his place in the stadium, Williams' coach stood, tears streaming from

Phil Edwards (left) and Brant Little (right) had previously run in the 800 meters semifinals. When Percy Williams wins the 100 meters race, they carry him the length of the grandstand.

Edna Robinson

his eyes. Around him, a large number of Dutch spectators had set up a turmoil of noise. They were happy that American boasts of winning the event had been dashed by a small runner from Canada. In one part of the arena, the chant of "Kan-a-da, Kan-a-da, Will-yams, Will-yams" could be heard. It began slowly at first, then gathered momentum like an enormous tidal wave, as one section after another took it up until the whole Olympic Stadium reverberated with the name of the Vancouver schoolboy and his country.

The tumult ended as the great audience rose and stood at attention for the victory ceremony. Unlike today, there was no podium on which the athletes stood, and the medals weren't awarded until the end of the Olympic Games. Instead, the victorious athletes faced the flagpoles as the banner of

The Canadian Red Ensign is hoisted on the center flagpole in honor of Williams' victory.

the champion's country was raised on the large center mast and those of the runners-up on the two poles on either side, while the national anthem of the victor was played. The Dutch bandmaster and his musicians didn't have the music for "O Canada" in Williams' honor, so they substituted "The Maple Leaf Forever." Like the start of the 100 meters, it took them three attempts before they got it right. And when they finally began, the Canadians found it hard going without the words. In that vast amphitheater, Marsh said, they made as much noise as a quartet of chickadees. Still, they did their best, despite singing off-key with voices choked with emotion.

The frenzy and excitement of Percy's victory carried into the dressing room. The Canadian girls' team burst in at an embarrassing moment and was rushed out by officials while he was draped in a dressing gown. After they were readmitted, the women mobbed and kissed him. "He never was kissed so often or so fast in his life and may never be again," Alex Gibb said. Fred

Marples, treasurer of the COC, and P.J. Mulqueen caught the fever. Instead of kissing Williams, they started with the girls' chaperone and finished with the youngest on the team. They played no favorites.

That evening, the celebration at the Holland House hotel for Percy was loud and unrestrained as large numbers of reporters and photographers competed for interviews and pictures. Meanwhile, at the Pension Regina, the atmosphere among the girls' team was one of quiet contentment. "Canada, are you satisfied with your daughters," Gibb asked rhetorically. They thought they would be the first to raise the Canadian flag over the Olympic Stadium, but Williams' victory had precluded it. Still, the placing of Bobbie, Myrtle, and Ethel in the final of the women's 100 meters was a source of pride. It was possible they might overshadow Percy's wonderful success by sweeping the event.

The president of the International Ice Hockey Federation arrived at their lodgings to convey his congratulations. He was followed by the Belgian fencing team, who came to serenade them. The appearance of players from the New Westminster Salmonbellies, Canada's team in the demonstration sport of lacrosse at the Olympics, carrying armloads of roses, was another pleasant surprise and contributed to the happy mood. For Alex Gibb, the acclamation of Canada's female athletes was a preview of a much larger celebration that would follow the 100 meters. She expected to see three Canadian flags flying from the official standards, and wondered where the Dutch Olympic officials would get them all. "We never once thought we weren't going to come in first," Jane Bell said.

Chapter Seven

Day of Heartbreak

"CANADA CONFIDENT ON THIRD DAY OF OLYMPIC CARNIVAL," Bobby Robinson announced in a newspaper article to Canadians back home on Tuesday, July 31. The overcast skies and falling rain that greeted the men's and women's track-and-field teams in the morning failed to dampen their mood. They were cheerful and impatient to begin. The beneficial effect of Percy Williams' championship on Canadian athletes, officials, and supporters was magnified by stories of the 100 meters, which filled European papers. Pictures showing the race and Percy being carried on the shoulders of his teammates covered the front pages. Any doubts about the quality of Canada's Olympic team had been convincingly dispelled.

Williams' victory was a glorious feat in itself, Robinson said, but it had also instilled a grim determination in the entire team. What the Vancouver schoolboy had done, others wanted to do. The enthusiasm produced by his success had spread to the women, spurring Myrtle, Ethel, and Bobbie to do well in the 100 meters final. Alex Gibb believed Myrtle and Bobbie had the best chances to win the event, but Ethel couldn't be counted out. The only question was their order of finish – first, second, or third?

As the Canadians looked forward to further triumphs, the Americans were in shock from the results of the previous day. Losses in the 400 meters hurdles and hammer throw to athletes from other countries had staggered them. And when Percy Williams won the sprint final, the American runners finishing fourth and sixth, the day of disaster was complete. The United States had never been worse than second in the event. Prior to the Games, the president of the American Olympic Committee, Major-General Douglas MacArthur, had predicted they had nine firsts sewed up. His forecast suddenly seemed hollow, and many were left wondering what was wrong with the American Olympic Team.

The Americans bucked up a little when sixteen-year-old Elizabeth Robinson qualified for the final in the 100 meters. The Illinois schoolgirl finished second to Rosenfeld in the first round, but amazed everyone by winning her semifinal heat, defeating the world record holder, Myrtle Cook, in doing it. Robinson's qualification was a surprise as she wasn't the team's best runner and wasn't expected to do well. Moreover, the Olympic Games were only her fourth track competition. Reporters had taken to calling her "Smiling Betty" because she always finished her race with a grin. She had now given her downhearted countrymen reason to smile. Hopefully, she would prevail in the sprint final and restore some respectability to the U.S. track team.

With three of the final six in the 100 meters wearing the Maple Leaf, a clean sweep of the event by Canada was a possibility. Yet Bobby Robinson believed that Myrtle, Bobbie, and the German, Helene "Leni" Schmidt, would fight it out for first place. The American, Elizabeth Robinson, the other German, Erna Steinberg, and Ethel Smith would come somewhere behind. Unlike the day before, the Canadian women had no problem finding a dressing room. Alex Gibb noted wryly that they could choose any one they wished as they had eliminated most of the other nations. She was in good spirits, pleased with the results of the team. "Our showing to date has made the Maple Leaf the outstanding emblem in Amsterdam," she boasted. "We can have everything except the crown jewels." Now, thirty minutes before the first women's track final at a modern Olympiad, the Canadians got ready.

★

Canada's Sports Hall of Fame

The pressure of competing at an Olympic Games affected Myrtle Cook and her running suffered. Her results in the preliminaries of the 100 meters, while satisfactory, were below expectations. Here, Bobby Robinson stands next to Myrtle.

For Myrtle Cook, it was a routine she knew well. It began at lunch at the Pension Regina, with a customary poached egg on toast and a large glass of water. Experience had taught her that a small quantity of food before a race was beneficial. Huge steaks were fine for rowers, but not for the average female athlete. In her room, she pulled out her equipment bag to check its contents. She believed in preparing for competition systematically, and began the ritual of checking off each part of her uniform to insure that nothing was missing.

Consulting the list pasted inside the lid of her bag, she verified that everything was at hand. Her two pairs of spiked shoes were there and, importantly, an extra pair of laces. Her uniform and sweat suit were packed inside, as were a pair of short running socks. Myrtle avoided high stockings because they required uncomfortable elastics to hold them up. She located the trowel for digging her starting holes and a vacuum flask. The latter was normally filled with hot tea or cocoa when she faced a long afternoon of running. But today it was unnecessary as only one race would be held. She usually put some sugar cubes in her bag as a source of energy, taking one a half hour before her event. Instead she would eat a square of Jersey Milk chocolate that was given the girls before their events. The stocktaking completed, Myrtle closed the bag and joined the others for the journey to the stadium.

The skies cleared at noon and the bright day augured well. The enthusiastic group of Canadian athletes was in good form as the bus drove through the streets of Amsterdam, past the canals, streetcars, and cyclists. The results of yesterday and the possibility of further triumphs, particularly in the women's 100 meters, heartened the team considerably. They sang and cheered wildly during the ride to the stadium, confident of a happy outcome to the day's events.

In the dressing room, everything was quiet as the women prepared. Myrtle said nothing to the others as she changed into her jersey and shorts. Following the example of some of the American girl athletes, she and Ethel Smith had cut off the sleeves of their tops for freer arm movement. As she dressed, she was pensive, her mind turning to the race ahead. She felt she must come through. It weighed on her as she struggled to master her fears and self-doubts. "It is not a good thing to make a world record just before competing in the Games," she admitted. "You become a target." As the world's record holder, she knew she was the fastest, and, if she ran as she did in Halifax, no one would catch her. Yet Amsterdam wasn't Halifax and the Olympic Stadium was much different than the Wanderers Grounds.

As the hour for the race approached, Alex Gibb and Marie Parkes tended to last-minute details. They fastened the competitors' numbers to the jerseys of the women. Gibb spoke some final words of advice as she and Parkes applied liniment and massaged the girls' legs. The rubdowns finished, the women pulled on their sweatpants and tops.

In silence they accompanied their manager down the long dark tunnel beneath the stands. The sounds of the stadium, at first a distant cacophony of noise, became increasingly louder and more distinct as they drew nearer to the entranceway to the field. Upon reaching the gate, Gibb wished them luck and departed.

Dazzled by the light, the girls emerged from the dark passageway into the stadium. As their eyes adapted to the brightness, they beheld a number of vibrant scenes: the German spectators waving hundreds of tiny tricolored flags of black, gold, and red; the distinctive larger banners of the various nations encircling the stadium; the massive scoreboard looming over it; the press section, conspicuous by its distinctive yellow hue, with dozens of reporters sitting behind tables pounding their typewriters; the competitors' section in red, where the other members of the girls' team were brandishing the Canadian Red Ensign; the emerald green infield surrounded by the red cinder track; and, at one end, the sight of women athletes competing in the discus throw.

The din created by the cheering and singing from those in the stands swelled about them as they walked to the infield. Removing their soft shoes, they put on their spikes and limbered up. In their previous races, an American had been the starter. For the final, a German was in charge. Two commands would precede the gun – *auf die Plätze!* meaning "on your marks," followed by *fertig,* indicating "set." Two false starts would result in disqualification.

Grabbing their trowels, the six athletes went to their lanes and began digging their holes behind the starting line. It would be twenty years before starting blocks appeared at the Olympics. Until then, runners would dig holes for their feet to push against and launch themselves forward when the gun sounded. On this afternoon of July 31, the contestants in the women's 100 meters final did the same. After trying the holes for depth and angle by practising a few starts, they removed their sweat suits and took their places on the track.

The Canadians were easily identifiable by their red shorts and white jerseys emblazoned with a red maple leaf and the word "Canada" on the front. Their outfits caused a mild sensation when the girls first appeared because their shorts rested a few inches above their knees, higher than those of the other female contestants. Not too high, though, as the length of women's track shorts was prescribed by a rule. Their jerseys, however, were another matter. They were so large that they billowed out over their shorts, like sails in a breeze. Whenever photographers wished to take a picture, the girls were forced to hike up their tops to show the Maple Leaf. Myrtle thought their costumes were awful.

The German starter gave the command, *"auf die Plätze!"* and the runners took their marks. The stadium fell silent as attention focused on the women crouched on the track. From where she was sitting, Jane thought Myrtle looked nervous. *"Fertig."* Then, as the crowd waited for the gun, one of six bolted and two shots were heard, signaling a false start. It was Myrtle Cook. She returned to the starting line and was warned by the starter. Again the women were commanded, *"auf die Plätze!"* then, *"fertig."* This time two runners left too soon and charged up the track until recalled by the gun. The spectators sagged in disappointment and the stadium buzzed over the second false start. The German Schmidt in lane two was one of the offenders and, to the consternation of the Canadians, the other in lane four was Myrtle.

The starter walked over, tapped her on the shoulder, and said, "Second break." She stood unbelieving for a moment, and then, realizing what it meant, burst into tears. As the crowd looked on in amazement, Myrtle slowly walked off the track.

"We were in shock," Jane said, for the Canadians never anticipated this outcome. They were still numb as the starter failed a third time to get the runners away. Schmidt had committed her second false start. When informed of her disqualification, the German athlete, instead of breaking into tears, shook her fist under the starter's nose, and the spectators feared they were about to witness a scene of face-scratching and hair-pulling. The perplexed official retreated a step and motioned Schmidt off the track. He then turned to Myrtle, who was sitting too near the starting line, sobbing uncontrollably. Afraid of the effect her crying would have on those remaining in the race, he persuaded the despondent Canadian to move behind the runners before he attempted to begin the race once more.

For Ethel Smith, Myrtle's disqualification was heartbreaking. "We were there to compete and win. That was the main thing," she said. For Myrtle, that opportunity was gone and Ethel knew what it meant to her teammate. "I looked back at Myrtle, she was standing behind and the tears were streaming down her face, and I thought, 'Oh my God, she's my friend and she's out of it.'" The distress caused by Myrtle's misfortune added to Smith's physical woes. She had been ill that morning, suffering severe cramps in her side. The false starts, disqualifications, and delays had rattled her. When she took her mark for the fourth time, her back leg was "shaking like crazy."

In lane six, Bobbie watched sadly as Myrtle left the track. She also realized they were at the Olympics to win. "Being first, second, or third is all that counts with the athlete," she said. "He doesn't know anything about him being a goodwill ambassador at all. That's a political thing." Unlike Myrtle, whose desire to win made her anxious before the start of every race, Bobbie thrived on high-pressured situations. "The one and only Bobby [Bobbie] Rosenfeld does her best in pinches," Phyllis Griffiths said, as one who watched and played against her, "and it is a cinch she won't let nervous tension get the better of her."

With the elimination of Schmidt and Cook, Bobbie was now clearly the favorite. She had beaten Ethel in the semifinal and Robinson in the first round. Steinberg, the other German, wasn't a threat and her times confirmed this. Nevertheless, Bobbie knew it was foolish to predict the outcome of a race. "I've seen girls come along who seemed to know every trick of the trade," she said, "girls who had dazzling speed and looked like invincibles. But tested in a gruelling contest, a lot of them would crack wide open." A slow starter, Bobbie didn't hit her stride until the 20 meters mark. She realized a good break at the beginning was essential. If trailing the leaders at the halfway mark, it must be by less than half a meter because she knew she had the power to drive for the last fifty and to challenge those in front. But in the "white-hot event" of the 100 meters, everything had to be perfect. Bobbie understood "the slightest mistake from start to finish . . . [meant] frustration." The command, *"auf die Plätze!"*, was given and she took her mark. Focusing on a spot eight inches in front of her, she waited. Then, *"fertig."*

The gun sounded and the fourth attempt to begin the race was a success. Ethel, in lane one, and Elizabeth Robinson, in lane five, broke quickly, followed by Bobbie and Erna Steinberg. The crowd rose to its feet with a roar and the stadium became a boiling cauldron of noise. For the first twenty-five meters, Ethel matched Robinson in speed and it was difficult to tell who was in front. By the halfway point, however, the American was ahead, Ethel was third, and Steinberg was fourth. But in the outside lane, in second place, Bobbie was flying and closing rapidly on the leader. Canadian and American supporters in the stands were frantically urging their athletes on as the gap between the two narrowed. By the three-quarters mark they appeared even, running stride for stride, and the arena was in a frenzy. Over the final

The finish of the women's 100 meters final shows (left to right) Rosenfeld (Canada), Robinson (United States), Steinberg (Germany), and Smith (Canada).

twenty-five meters, it was impossible to tell who was leading and, when both runners hit the string at the finish line, it seemed the race was a dead heat. Less than a yard behind, Ethel was third, followed by Steinberg.

"Was I first or second?" Bobbie asked, at the end of the race. The officials picking the order of the finishers couldn't say. The close contest forced them to huddle in an effort to agree upon the placement of the first two. The German judge, calling first, named Elizabeth Robinson as the winner. But the French judge, responsible for second, also picked the American, which meant he felt Bobbie was first. The English judge agreed. The chief judge, who was American, resolved the conflict by placing Robinson first and Bobbie second. When the results were announced, Jane and the other Canadians were surprised. They thought that either Bobbie or Ethel was first, not the American. They weren't alone.

Alice Milliat, president of the *Fédération Sportive Féminine Internationale*, was on the field for the women's 100 meters, looking after the interests of the competitors. She watched the finish and was sure Bobbie was the winner. She agreed with the French and English judges that Robinson broke the tape with her arms and not with her body, as required by the rules. It happened that Bobby Kerr was also a judge for the race, calling fifth place. But when the contestants were reduced to four because of disqualifications, he reckoned his role as an official had ended. For this reason, he refused to become involved in the discussion. Yet Kerr felt the Canadian officials should know about the judges' disagreement, especially as the English official and Milliat strongly believed the dispute was one for an impartial jury to consider.

Meanwhile, unaware of the difference among the judges over first place, Bobbie and Ethel returned to Myrtle, who was sitting near the starting line, her head buried in her arms and her body shaking with sobs. They sat with their arms about her, but she was inconsolable. Her dream of personal glory gone, nothing they could say or do would soothe her. Afterwards, a shakened Myrtle walked out of the stadium dressed in her tracksuit, found a bench by a canal, sat down, and cried some more. Returning to the arena sometime later, she made her lonely trek through the dark passageway under the stands to the dressing room. "It is at the door of the tunnel," Myrtle said, "that your coach, manager, chaperone, or best friend pats you on the back and whispers, 'Go to it, kid, you can do it!' Sometimes you do and [you] come back through the tunnel treading on air. If you fail, well you still have to come back, and the journey seems blacker than ever."

Jane and the others tried to soften the blow of her disqualification by telling her that perhaps it was for the best. "We told her, and we all felt the same," Jane said, "'maybe you were lucky that you had the false breaks. What if you had run and hadn't come first? You would have felt a whole lot worse than not being able to have competed.'" It made little difference to Myrtle. She still wanted to be the winner, but it would never be. Her hopes of Olympic glory had been forever dashed by the second false start. "Myrtle didn't want to talk to anybody or have anything to do with anybody," Jane said. She was devastated.

Myrtle blamed her elimination on extreme nervousness and commands given in a foreign language. Her friend and teammate, Ethel Smith, also attributed the disqualification to the German starter, but for a different reason. Myrtle was used to the man who started the races at most of the Toronto meets, Ethel said. He would give them lots of time to get on their marks and, after he commanded, "Get set," he would wait two seconds and then fire the gun. Myrtle was used to this pattern and knew when to break. In Amsterdam, however, it was different. Unaccustomed to other starters, she was breaking too soon. Bobby Robinson had warned her that if she did it twice in competition, they would disqualify her. His warning proved prophetic. Alex Gibb, who knew how badly Myrtle wanted an Olympic title, said, "She saw ahead of her down a lane of a hundred yards and a little more, a world's championship glittering on that slender woollen tape blowing idly in the wind." She was too eager and it cost her. The sight of Myrtle standing behind the starting line, an amazed look on her face and tears welling up in her eyes, was one Gibb never forgot.

As the premier track event for women, the 100 meters final provided an unfamiliar aspect to the Games and was watched with interest. The appearance of female competitors in an Olympic track final for the first time, the unexpected disqualifications, and the reactions of Cook and Schmidt were almost as compelling as the race itself. The correspondent for the *New York Times* described them as "scenes entirely feminine, and never before witnessed in any Olympic Stadium." But a dissimilar and unpleasant exhibition involving Canadian officials was soon to follow. It provoked such a row that one newspaper was moved to recommend a shipment of muzzles and a crew of highly trained muzzlers be sent the next time the Canadian Olympic Committee went abroad.

Once the American was declared the winner of the women's 100 meters, Bobby Kerr went to Bobby Robinson and told him about the judges' disagreement. Kerr also repeated Alice Milliat's comments that the disputed finish was one for the jury to consider. After listening to Kerr, and convinced

Edna Robinson

After the American was announced as the winner of the women's 100 meters, Bobby Robinson wrote out a protest. He was still fuming over the flag-raising ceremony for Percy Williams' victory the day before. It had taken some time before a Canadian flag could be found and, when it went up on the center flagpole, it was a small banner instead of a customary large one.

that Rosenfeld was first, Robinson hurriedly wrote out a protest. Then he, Dr. A.S. Lamb, P.J. Mulqueen, and Alex Gibb proceeded across the field to the jury stand to make it official. Neither Mulqueen nor Gibb was hopeful the action would succeed. It was done more to show that the Canadian officials were on their toes and would fight for the rights of their athletes. The morale of the women's team was at stake, Mulqueen was convinced, and the protest was necessary to uphold it. Alex Gibb agreed. "What would have been said if I had come back to Canada and had not fought for their rights?" she asked.

Reaching the officials' stand, Gibb informed them, as manager of the Canadian women's team, she wished to file a protest. She presented the paper and paid the necessary fee. At that point, Dr. Lamb turned to Mulqueen and indicated he disagreed with the action. For Lamb, the protest violated his sense of sportsmanship. Nevertheless, Mulqueen insisted that it should be lodged. Lamb then told the others he was disassociating himself from them and their protest.

Stunned by Lamb's announcement, and embarrassed by the show of disunity before the jury men, Gibb believed all was lost. She felt they should have presented a solid Canadian front. The fiery Mulqueen was beside himself. He accused Lamb of "pussyfooting, playing to the gallery, and playing politics." The protest was the right thing to do, the president of the COC maintained. "I stood behind the team that I had associated myself with," he said. "I stood behind the team and for the morale of the team, rather than for any silly idea that it was a crime to protest."

But Lamb felt it was an unhappy episode that reflected badly on all Canadians. A month before, he said that if Canada's contribution to the Olympics was raising the standard of the Games, then winning was only incidental. To his sorrow, he discovered that not everyone agreed. He regretted lacking the courage to insist the protest not be filed. Yet he felt a heated discussion between himself and Mulqueen before the International Jury would have been even more shameful. "May we always be able to accept defeat with grace and fortitude," he said, "to respect the final decision of the judges

Canadian Olympic Committee

Dr. A.S. Lamb, manager of the Canadian Olympic Team, accompanied Robinson, Mulqueen, and Gibb to the jury stand, believing they were there on another matter. Upon learning they were protesting the result of the women's 100 meters race, he disassociated himself.

and to confine our winning to the cinder path and not the committee room."

In Canada, the newspapers gave special prominence to the controversy. "CANADA PROTESTS DEFEAT OF FANNY ROSENFELD" proclaimed the headline in the *Toronto Daily Star*. The *Vancouver Sun*'s front page declared, "CANADA PROTESTS WOMEN'S RACE." The Canadian action touched a nerve, and debate among sportswriters, editorial writers, and the public was heated. Mike Rodden of the *Globe* observed it was sad the Canadian officials saw fit to protest, particularly as protests weren't popular in Canada, where athletes knew how to win and also how to lose. Phyllis Griffiths agreed. "I think protests have very little place in sport," she said. "The attitude of Dr. Lamb, president of the Amateur Athletic Union of Canada, in refusing to support the protest is significant to say the least." In Montreal, Lamb's hometown, Elmer Ferguson of the *Herald* deplored the protest, and complimented Lamb for his fine sense of dignity and sportsmanship. Yet the Toronto *Evening*

Telegram's Ted Reeve cautioned his readers not to be too hard on the Canadians for protesting. "It's nice to be a 'good sport,'" he said. "But the fighting spirit necessary to produce good athletes will let out an occasional yelp when it is being tramped on too crudely."

Disappointed they didn't win the 100 meters, the women's team sadly accepted the result and agreed with Dr. Lamb's actions. "Mr. Lamb who was the manager of the team felt it wasn't in Olympic tradition to protest," Bobbie said. "I guess he was right." Jane was more outspoken: "I thought the protest was unsportsmanlike and was against the Olympic oath." Myrtle Cook felt the same. "I think if every athlete will repeat it [the Olympic oath] to herself on every occasion of competition, it will help materially in forming a clearer idea of sportsmanship."

At the Pension Regina that evening, thoughts of Olympic oaths, sportsmanship, playing the game, and all the rest were cold comfort to a miserable Myrtle Cook and the others. "We began to wonder," Jane said, "are we so great?" A pall hung over the Canadian women's team and Alex Gibb admitted that things weren't as bright at their hotel as they had hoped. Let down by the second- and third-place finishes in an event she was certain they would win, shocked by Cook's disqualification, and unhappy with Lamb's refusal to support the protest, Alex Gibb was in a somber mood. There was comfort of sorts in the fact that Canada had placed three of its four runners in the final and Bobbie had pushed winner Elizabeth Robinson to a world's record. "It is difficult for those in Canada to realize the different conditions under which the girls have to compete here," Gibb said. "The strain is a terrific one, the starters speak in a foreign language – German today – all sorts of imaginary ills and pains crop up with the high tension." Nevertheless, she commended the women for their team spirit and good sportsmanship, which had made them favorites with the Dutch.

In spite of losing a close race, Bobbie Rosenfeld was feeling better because of what Joe Wright Sr., coach of the Canadian rowing team, said to her afterwards. He came out of his seat in the stands to meet her as she was making her way to the competitors' section. Putting his arm around her in a fatherly fashion, he told her that he was right on the finish line of the race and, in his opinion, she had won it. "I don't care what the judges think," he said, "I'll always think of you as the winner of the 100 meters." His words removed the sting she felt from the defeat and lifted her spirits.

But for another, the memory burned. That night, after what Bobby Robinson called the most heartbreaking day in Olympic history, alone in her room, Myrtle Cook cried herself to sleep.

Chapter Eight

Remarkable Sportsmanship

The next morning, after a good night's rest, all of the girls except Myrtle felt better. Despite the heavy rain and the news they had lost the 100 meters protest by a vote of 3-1, they were upbeat. The 800 meters and the relay still remained and they were determined to show Europe they could run by winning both. If Jean's injured leg stood up, Alex Gibb was certain she would do well in her heat that afternoon. In addition, the performances of Bobbie, Ethel, Myrtle, and Jane in the 100 meters boded well for the women's relay trials on Saturday. "We still had the relay," Jane said. "We came second and third in the 100 meters. We were sure to win."

The heavy morning showers stopped at noon, but a light drizzle prevented the sodden track from drying. Despite the unfavorable conditions, both Percy Williams and Hamilton's Johnny Fitzpatrick qualified for the final of the 200 meters later in the day. Their results were a tonic, improving everyone's mood and raising hopes for the heats of the women's 800 meters. Jean Thompson, the baby of the squad, was a favorite in the event and the Canadians were optimistic.

Privately, however, the manager of the girls' team was worried. The Penetang athlete's injury, her enforced rest, and their effects concerned Alex Gibb. "Bed is not the place to prepare for a test of this kind," Gibb remarked.

There was an additional worry. Jean was suffering from a case of nerves so severe, it appeared she might not compete. Realizing that something had to be done, Gibb discussed the matter with Robinson and Kerr. She then went to Bobbie Rosenfeld with a request. They wanted her to go in the 800 meters as moral support for Jean.

Although Bobbie was a sprinter and field athlete, she had run the longer distance at the Ontario Olympic Trials and at a meet in Hamilton afterwards. But that was almost a month ago, and since coming overseas she had practised only the discus and 100 meters. "Are you crazy," a disbelieving Rosenfeld said, in response to Gibb's appeal, "me in the 800 meters?" She was being asked to enter an Olympic event for which she hadn't trained, and to face world-class runners who were fresh. But after Gibb explained that Jean was a bundle of nerves, and she needed bolstering in the event, Bobbie relented. "Alright, I'll go in and lend her a little moral support," she said. "But don't expect anything from me because that's not my distance at all."

Alex Gibb knew she was taking a risk, but Jean's emotional and physical state left her no choice. She was hopeful that Bobbie's ability as an all-round athlete would compensate for a lack of experience and training. Moreover, Gibb liked the odds. Only five runners were entered in Bobbie's heat, and the first three would qualify for the final. Bobbie wisely laid off the fast early pace, gauged her stamina and speed, and on the final lap moved from last to third to qualify easily. Remarking on Bobbie's versatility, the sports editor of the *Evening Telegram* said, "This Toronto girl is one of those natural athletes so rare these days who is as good as the best in anything she undertakes, athletics, hockey, basketball, baseball." In the competitors' section following the race, she was hugged by her teammates. If Jean could do the same, their day would be complete.

Jean's heat was the third and final one. Encouraged by Bobbie's effort, she took to the line, intent on doing well. At the sound of the gun, she broke quickly to the front. After one lap she led by six yards, the ten runners behind her strung out in single file. During the second and final lap, the runners gradually closed up, but Thompson increased her speed to maintain a safe

Jean Thompson is shown winning her heat in the 800 meters. Florence McDonald of the United States is second. Thompson's victory was a relief to Alex Gibb, who feared the teenager's injury, evident by her bandaged left leg, would hamper her chances.

National Archives of Canada/PA151008

lead. A final charge by the American Florence McDonald and the German Elfriede Wewer down the homestretch caused an outburst of cheers, but the Canadian ran away from them, comfortably finishing in front.

Afterwards, Alex Gibb felt better about their prospects. Jean showed no ill effects from her injury and time away from training. In addition, she seemed to have conquered her nerves. Best of all, two of her girls were in the final. Bobbie's qualification meant company for Jean, someone to settle her down, if necessary, and hopefully inspire her to win the team's first championship. If anyone could do it, Bobbie could. In Amsterdam, she had emerged as the leader of the girls' contingent. "She was the backbone of the whole team," Jane said, "and so much fun to be with." Whenever anything needed smoothing out, she usually looked after it by saying or doing something humorous.

So far, it was a good afternoon's work. Williams and Fitzpatrick were running in the 200 meters final still to come, and Thompson and Rosenfeld had qualified for tomorrow's 800 meters final. The promise of more points looked bright and the Canadians were delighted.

But not everyone was happy. Following the 100 meters protest, Dr. Lamb suspected it was only a matter of time before "another cyclonic outburst" from Robinson and Mulqueen would occur. His fears were soon realized. During the final heat of the women's 800 meters, a teammate of American runner Florence McDonald was observed on the grass infield pacing McDonald the length of the homestretch. This was a clear breach of rules and cause for disqualification. P.J. Mulqueen and Bobby Robinson located the president of the IAAF, J.S. Edstrom, and told him of the incident. He promised to look into it. But when he came back and stated it was the Canadian girl who was paced, Mulqueen exploded. "Don't insult my intelligence," he said. "Why should an American girl pace a Canadian girl?" After further investigation, Edstrom confirmed Mulqueen and Robinson's charges. He told them that the offending American was warned by the judges and promised it wouldn't happen again.

The assurance failed to mollify the Canadian officials, who felt stronger action was warranted. To them, it was a mere slap on the wrist and another example of partiality. An irate Robinson complained that Canadian athletes were penalized for violating the rules while other athletes got away with infractions just as glaring. The charge was given added weight during the men's pole vault competition. Because of an error on the part of the Dutch officials, there was a mix-up in competitors' numbers, and Canada's hope in the event, Vic Pickard, reached the jumping pit late. When he asked for a practise jump, he was refused by the American official in charge. After this same official was observed openly coaching an American competitor, Pickard called Dr. Lamb's attention to it. Yet no action was taken by the Olympic officials. The Canadian finished fourth in the competition.

★

Edna Robinson

Percy Williams smiles for the camera following the 200 meters race. On the photograph he has written: "To Bobby Robinson. A real sport and a good manager. (Remember the boat home) Always, Percy Williams, 100 & 200 M., Olympics 1928."

While the behavior of the Canadian officials divided their ranks in Amsterdam and stirred up a tempest at home, the athletes went about the business of competing. The qualification of Percy Williams for the 200 meters final raised hopes for a second championship, something no one imagined at the beginning of the Olympics. The elusive "double" in the 100 and 200 meters had been achieved only twice before, in 1904 and 1912. The final would be Percy's eighth race in four days, a heavy workload for even the most experienced runners. Still, the impressive manner in which he advanced through the three preliminary rounds had shown his ability to face the strain.

Moreover, if the frail-looking, 126-pound Vancouver schoolboy was bothered about his chances against men who were bigger and fresher, he kept those concerns to himself. "He does not worry," Bobby Robinson said.

At 3:50 P.M., the final of the men's 200 meters was announced over the stadium's loudspeakers. The girls' team watched from the stands as Williams stripped down. They chaffed at the exasperating slowness with which he removed his sweatpants and top. Someone said he would be rushed at the mark, but he took it calmly. The command, *"fertig,"* was given by the German starter. Against a backdrop of low hanging clouds, smoke from the Marathon Tower drifting lazily over the stadium and the flags drooping in the fine rain, the six sprinters crouched at the starting line. The gun sounded and all broke together. Unlike the 100 meters, the first start was perfect, and the girls strained to see who was leading as the runners charged up their lanes. The staggered start made it impossible to tell.

As they came out of the turn and began the straight stretch to the finish, a clearer picture emerged. The girls could see the German, American, and

Edna Robinson

Percy Williams wins the 200 meters and his second gold medal at the Olympic Games. Johnny Fitzpatrick, the other Canadian in the race, is at the far left.

English runners fighting Williams for the lead. Fifty yards from the tape, it looked as though the German or Englishman would win it. But, at that moment, Percy changed gears and accelerated. His speed carried him ahead of the pack, and he crossed the finish line the clear winner by almost a yard. Johnny Fitzpatrick, the other Canadian, was fifth. In the competitors' stands, half a dozen excited Canadians broke past policemen, climbed over the railing, rolled down the banked cycling track, and ran towards the champion. Upon reaching him, two of them swooped the diminutive athlete up shoulder-high and paraded him in front of the cheering throng. And when he arrived at the competitors' section afterwards, he was mobbed by the

Edna Robinson

While other Canadian athletes look on, two of Percy's teammates hoist him up after his victory, waving small Canadian flags in celebration. Moments later, the Canadian Red Ensign, sent down by the girls, was draped over his shoulders.

Canadians. Among them was Vic Pickard, who was amazed at what he had just witnessed. He didn't know where Williams got his speed and how he ever won both the 100 and 200 meters races, but Percy was a marvel.

"Well, what are you going to win this afternoon?" was the greeting given the Canadians by spectators in the Olympic Stadium on Thursday, August 2, the fifth day of competition. Yesterday's victory by Williams was a popular one. When the Canadian flag was raised on the center pole, it was greeted by loud cheering from the multitude. On this day, a large crowd was present for the stadium events. The weather proved cooperative, and the drizzle of the previous twenty-four hours had been replaced by overcast skies. Once again, the Canadians began well, as four of them qualified for the second round of the men's 400 meters later in the day. Yet for supporters of the Maple Leaf, the highlight of the program was the women's 800 meters final.

Shortly before 3:45 P.M., the nine finalists appeared on the field. Of the five events on the women's program, this was the most controversial. The length of the race – two laps of the track – troubled many, who felt it placed too much strain and stress on the competitors. During the preliminary heats the day before, the correspondent for *Le Figaro* observed the exhausted state of the French contestants at the finish and worried the distance compelled young women to efforts beyond their means. Another account described Florence McDonald staggering across the finish line in a dangerously fatigued condition. Now, as the contestants stood waiting for the gun, many in the crowd were apprehensive.

When the gun sounded, Jean started strongly and took the early lead. On the backstretch of the first lap, however, she was overtaken by two Germans, running at a furious pace, and dropped to third. Several seconds later, at the beginning of the final lap, she fell to fourth when the Swedish runner passed her. Jean had never been behind in the 800 meters before, but she wasn't worried. Half of the race still remained, more than enough to catch the leaders. She held her position until the backstretch. Then, making her move, she accelerated and went after those in front. Passing one of the Germans, she bore down on the Swede, who was in second place. Simultaneously, Japanese competitor Kinuye Hitomi, running behind Jean, began her charge for the leaders. As she surged forward and came even with the Canadian, her swinging arms accidentally struck Jean, giving her a nasty surprise and a stiff jostle. The shock seemed to take something out of the young athlete. Rounding the final curve, with only one hundred meters left, Jean was in fourth place, but she was fading badly and the American McDonald was gaining.

From the stands, Jane and the others watched the drama unfold. "The Japanese girl who was behind came up and almost tripped Jean, enough to put her off her stride," Jane said. "All of a sudden, when they got to where the 100 meters starts, Bobbie came up. She was going straight out and was catching everybody. We thought, 'You know, she's going to come ahead.' She came up beside Jean and she never passed her." In the press section, Bobby Robinson stared in wonder as Rosenfeld, who had trailed the field all the way, came with a rush from last place, passed the four competitors in front of her, and drew even with Jean. He saw her running alongside, talking to her. Jean seemed to recover, picked herself up, and finished fourth, with Bobbie right behind.

There was no doubt in Robinson's mind that Bobbie could have finished ahead of Jean. Others, such as Jane, were convinced she could have done even better. Yet Bobbie always saw her role in the 800 meters as a supporting one. This was Jean's event and she was the star. As such, Bobbie intended to stay far behind during the race, out of the spotlight. But the jostle given Jean, and its effect, changed everything. She realized that third was impossible for Jean: The Swedish runner was too far ahead. But Bobbie was determined the young athlete would finish fourth. For the rest of the race she remained at Jean's shoulder, encouraging her. As they approached the finish line Bobbie dropped behind, allowing Jean to finish in front. To come ahead of her was never an option. "That was the sporting thing to do," Phyllis Griffiths said. "It gave Canada the points just the same and gave the seventeen-year-old Penetang girl the extra bit of glory in her special event."

The finish of the women's 800 meters final shows Radke (Germany) first, Hitomi (Japan) second, and Gentzel (Sweden) third. Jean Thompson can be glimpsed behind the Swedish runner.

Immediately following the race, Bobbie placed her arm on Jean's shoulder and tried to console the heartbroken runner. Since competing in the 800 meters, the Penetang athlete had never been jostled or beaten in a race. Despondent over her result, she slumped to the ground in tears. Bobbie dropped down beside her, to comfort her. Not far away, another athlete was lying on the infield, crying bitterly. The Japanese girl, upset with her second-place finish, had thrown herself on the grass. The other runners moved to the infield, sat down to catch their breath, and waited for the judges to decide the placings.

The sight of three women in apparent difficulty and others sitting on the infield breathing heavily confirmed the worst fears of those who believed the event was too much for women to bear. Male reporters described in extravagant detail what they witnessed. The correspondent for the Toronto *Evening Telegram* said that both Canadian girls, the Japanese, and others "keeled over" on the grass in a distressing manner after the finish, but were quickly revived. In a similar vein, the writer for the *New York Times* reported that six of the nine runners were completely exhausted at the finish and fell headlong on the ground. Several had to be carried off the track. The reporter for *Le Figaro* found it to be an "ugly looking spectacle," and the London *Times* correspondent added that the half-dozen prostrate and obviously distressed forms lying on the grass at the side of the track after the race was a warning for women's athletics in general.

The female perspective of the race was noticeably different. Jane Bell, who trained for the 800 meters, never found the distance a problem. "People who ran the 800 [in Amsterdam] didn't think it was difficult," she said. "I'm sure no one thought it was hard. It was just those officials who thought so." Myrtle Cook, who watched the race, agreed, and described the incidence of runners collapsing at the finish as "grossly exaggerated." She didn't see one single case of actual distress among the girls, she said, and the condition of the women at the end of the race was no different from that of the men in the same event. Alex Gibb, incensed over the way the race was reported, refused to let "a few old fogies" change her mind concerning the event or women's participation at the Olympic Games.

The strongest testament came from Bobbie herself. "Any girl who satisfactorily passes a medical examination and who accepts and practises correct methods of training is capable of running eight hundred meters," she said. "The German and Japanese entries . . . did not experience any difficulty in the distance race, and even though I had not trained specially for it, there was no undue effort required to enable me to finish." Furthermore, the 800 meters final was Bobbie's fifth race in four days.

★

Because of her performances in the 100 and 800 meters, Bobbie became a favorite of European reporters, who sought to know more about her. As usual, she downplayed her feats by making light of them. When the correspondents asked her about training, she saw an opportunity to have some fun. She told them she practised only twice a week because, at 120 pounds, she lacked the stamina to do more. Then, with a twinkle in her eye, she added that she needed at least two pints of beer a day to maintain her strength.

Jean's defeat was one more setback for the Canadian women's Olympic team. Coming two days after the disappointment of the 100 meters, the 800 meters was another unhappy outcome. Yet the German who was victorious achieved a remarkable time, breaking the world's record by seven seconds. Bobby Robinson admitted that Jean at her best couldn't have won. He was certain, however, she could have finished third, or as high as second, had her injury not confined her to bed for a week. Lou Marsh put the race in perspective when he said that more runners were behind Jean and Bobbie at the finish than there were in front of them. "Penetang need feel no pangs of disgrace over Jean Thompson," he added, "and Toronto should certainly feel no disgrace over Fanny Rosenfeld."

The 800 meters result was discouraging, but Jean and Bobbie had done their best. A top-three finish would have been wonderful, but a fourth and fifth were still commendable. As Bobby Robinson put it, anybody in the first six at the Olympics was considered a champion. Moreover, Bobbie's act in helping Jean complete the race and letting her cross the finish line in front was a source of pride for them all. Alex Gibb described it as "one of the finest exhibitions of sportsmanship ever witnessed on any track." Jane felt the same. "Of course, we were terribly disappointed for Jean," she said. "But the loss was overshadowed by the wonderful gesture and sportsmanlike thing that Bobbie had done."

At the Pension Regina that evening, everyone regretted Jean's loss. The dispirited runner was sorry she hadn't done what she wanted. Yet the disappointment felt by the team was tempered by the knowledge that Jean's injury and suspension of training handicapped her for the final. And when she was jostled by the Japanese runner, it seemed like one more piece of bad luck, which doomed her chance for victory. Everyone agreed the bump was unfortunate, but there were no hard feelings. Although they hadn't won two of the events they were favored to win, the relay and high jump still remained. "We just took our punches and went on," Jane said, after the 800 meters race. "Ethel Smith and I thought, 'Well, that's too bad that it happened. But that's not going to make any difference in the relay.'"

Chapter Nine

The "Matchless Six"

I f Jane Bell considered the relay as the final opportunity for the runners to show their stuff, Myrtle Cook saw the race as her last chance for personal atonement. For three nights following her disqualification she had cried herself to sleep, haunted by the feeling of letting the team down. A victory in the relay would lessen the pain of the 100 meters and allow her to regain some self-esteem. But Myrtle knew the race was full of hazards and speed didn't guarantee success.

The usual arrangement in a sprint relay is the fastest member runs last, and the next fastest, who must also be a good starter, leads off. A skilled baton handler and straightaway runner is second, and a good baton handler and curve runner is third. Although Myrtle, Ethel, Bobbie, and Jane were all veteran relay runners, they had never competed together as a team. The closest they came was at the Millrose Games a few months earlier, when all of them, except Bobbie, were part of the winning relay squad. In Amsterdam, it wasn't until the first day in the training stadium that they fixed the order in the relay. Jane initiated the discussion. "I don't care where anybody else goes," she said, "but I'm going to run the third leg because it's on the corner, and if I'm behind I'd rather chase somebody." Myrtle said she would be the anchor. When Ethel indicated she didn't want to start, it was decided: She would run second and Bobbie would begin.

The manner in which everything was arranged seemed haphazard, but the girls were used to the order at home. Myrtle was the anchor and Ethel the second on the Canadian Ladies' relay team. Jane was familiar with the third position, having run it at the Millrose Games. As for Bobbie, leading off was something she knew from her time with the famous Canadian National Exhibition squad.

Their positions decided, the girls spent the week before the Olympics practising the proper method of gripping the baton, passing it while running at full speed, and receiving it with the right hand on the hip, palm upwards. Under Bobby Kerr's watchful eye, they soon achieved the machinelike exchanges essential for success. And when they took their places for the first heat of the 4 x 100 meters relay, they were ready.

The afternoon of Saturday, August 4, the seventh day of the Olympic Games, was spoiled by a steady downpour of rain, which gave the track the appearance of an Irish bog. A strong wind was also blowing, diminishing any hopes that records would be set. Despite the weather, a large crowd was there for the relay trials, 3,000 meters steeplechase, and the decathlon. By the time of the heats for the women's 4 x 100 meters, conditions were so miserable that the contestants were reluctant to remove their sweat suits. In the competitors' section, Alex Gibb fretted that the Canadians might be overanxious to make up for the loss in the 100 meters. Yet the sight of Bobbie Rosenfeld at the starting line was reassuring, for she knew that in Bobbie they had a lead-off runner who was "as steady as a rock."

Whatever worries Gibb had before the race were gone by the end of the first 100 meters as Bobbie's quick start and strong running had given the team a three-yard advantage. Ethel added three more to the lead and Jane another one. Then Myrtle, tearing down the stretch "like a young whirlwind," gained an additional five yards. Their victory over teams from Holland, France, and Sweden was achieved with ridiculous ease. Moreover, on a day of bitter wind and cold rain, "the flying four" had established a world's record of 49⅖ seconds when none was expected. Bobby Robinson noted that every one of the girls ran like a champion and their baton-passing was the best of the afternoon. It appeared the Canadian women were about to win their first Olympic title.

If hopes for a victory in the relay were high, the expectations for the women's high jump were just as promising, for Ethel Catherwood – the most photographed female athlete at the Olympic Games – would be in action. Many reckoned the contest would be between her, a South African, and a German. Yet Phyllis Griffiths was confident the Saskatoon Lily could jump 5 feet 4 inches, or better – good enough to win. Nevertheless, Griffiths asked Canadians to pray the United States didn't pull a surprise with a girl high jumper like Elizabeth Robinson in the 100 meters.

With two events remaining, the women's team still had an excellent chance of winning the track-and-field championship of the world. Although no Canadians had competed in the discus, their results in the 100 and 800 meters had put them in third place with 14 points – four behind Germany, and two behind the United States. Griffiths felt the Germans were their chief opposition and that even if Ethel failed to win her event but beat her German rival, it would be enough to win the title. For Griffiths was certain the wearers of the Maple Leaf, with their record-breaking performance in the relay, couldn't lose. Like many Canadians, she had been unhappy with their results so far. "It's about time Canada won first place in a feminine event," she complained. "The relay and the high jump are the only things remaining on the program, and a 'double first' would finish it off in great style."

That night, a happy Bobby Robinson went to bed confident that, in less than twenty-four hours, Canada's athletes would add to their already impressive record. He had forecast that the Amsterdam Olympics would witness the greatest effort ever made by representatives of Canada. Their results thus far hadn't proven him wrong and, on the final day of competition, they seemed ready to confirm his prediction wholeheartedly. Besides the women, the men had qualified for the 400 and 1600 meters relay finals, and the prospect for the marathon was promising. At the Pension Regina, Jane was also thinking of tomorrow. "We knew what we were supposed to do," she said. "This was it."

On Sunday, the final day of track-and-field competition at the ninth Olympiad, the girls' quarters were a hubbub of activity as the team prepared for the afternoon's events. They had arisen early to heavy, watery skies, but the prospect of a gloomy day did little to affect their mood. They were still excited by their world's record in the relay, set the day before, and were certain that, by competition's end, the elusive Olympic victory would finally be theirs. Also, after a week of waiting, Ethel would begin her quest for high-jumping supremacy. When the bus arrived to take them to the Olympic Stadium, the women discovered the men in similar spirits, and a happy band of athletes journeyed to the scene of competition for the last time.

By two o'clock, the start of the day's contests, it was only 61° Fahrenheit. The overcast skies prevented the temperature from rising, and a strong wind made the day even colder. Reluctant to remove their sweat tops and pants, the athletes sought additional protection against the elements. Jane and Ethel wrapped themselves in their purple capes of the Parkdale Ladies' Athletic Club. After these proved inadequate, they grabbed the flaming red Hudson's Bay blankets, which had been given to the team before the Olympics. Fortunately, on this cool and cloudy day, the girls didn't have long to wait. The preliminary round of the running high jump and the women's relay final were the first events on the program.

Interest in the relay race was keen because the teams from Canada, Germany, and the United States were in the final. The unhappy circumstances surrounding the 100 meters four days earlier remained fresh. The disqualifications of two runners and the controversial finish between two others left many wondering who was the fastest woman in the world. A rerun of the event to settle the issue had been suggested, but the Americans refused to consider it. The relay final was a chance to answer the question.

For three of the four principal players in the 100 meters drama – Cook, Schmidt, and Robinson – were all running the anchor leg for their teams. If all three received the baton at the same time for the final one hundred meters, then the argument over sprinting supremacy would be settled at last.

Although the Canadians had set a world's record the day before and were the favorites to win, Alex Gibb was nervous. Thoughts of the 100 and 800 meters weighed on her mind. Would something unforeseen happen to affect the outcome of the relay? Would a rival team come out of nowhere and spoil their chances? They were also running out of time, and only two events remained for them to fulfill earlier predictions of Olympic success. They needed to show their mettle.

As the start of the relay approached, nerves were taut. In the competitors' stand, Gibb found it almost unbearable to watch the girls come onto the field, wrap themselves in their Hudson's Bay blankets, and then take a few leg stretches. Among the women, the pressure was equally intense. "We were keen to win because of Myrtle's previous disqualification," Jane said. For Ethel Smith, the incentive was greater. "We gotta win," she said. "Everything was for Canada. Not so much yourself. Canada came first."

When the official arrived with the numbers in a hat to determine lane selection, Bobbie Rosenfeld made a flying dive to get into the hat first. Looking at the number, she was jubilant. She had drawn the inside lane. "We in the stand knew it immediately," Alex Gibb said, "because she got so excited she jumped up and down and held her hand high in the air with one finger so that we would know the Canadians were getting a break in the luck at last." Not only would Bobbie be closest to the starter and hear the gun immediately, she, Ethel, Jane, and Myrtle could see the other runners and know if they were ahead or behind.

Before separating to take their places on the track, the girls embraced and wished each other luck. Jane tried to strike up a conversation with the German and Italian runners as her group was escorted to the starting point for those running the third leg of the race. During the Games, the absence of an Olympic village isolated athletes in their accommodations. Language also hampered socializing. "We liked the Polish girls," Myrtle said, "but gave up trying to juggle their names on [our] tongues." Jane's attempts to communicate with the German and Italian athletes proved just as hopeless. She had better luck with the American girl, whom she knew from the Millrose Games. The conversation ended when the official directed Jane to her spot on the inside lane. She watched the others move off and take their positions. Looking about, she was struck by the sounds of the stadium and the colorful spectacle it presented. A small group of Canadians was easily discernable in the competitors' stand by their sweat suits with the word "CANADA" on them. Someone was waving P.J. Mulqueen's large Canadian Red Ensign. Throughout the arena, smaller flags of various countries were being flourished by the noisy throng, their multicolored banners vibrant beneath the gray skies.

Nearby the other runners paced nervously, anxious for the race to start. For an impressionable eighteen-year-old, standing in a foreign stadium thousands of miles from home, and an Olympic final only seconds away, the effect was profound. "It's hard to explain exactly the feeling you have," Jane said. "You know what the feeling is, and you feel it only occasionally again. But you never forget that real explosion of excitement."

Looking down, she saw her bandaged leg and recalled the shin splint she had suffered the week before. As the slowest runner on the relay team, Jane knew she was the weak link, and her injury heightened the fact. She surprised everyone by advancing to the semifinals in the 100 meters, only to be eliminated by an error in judgment. But doubts remained, and she saw the relay as her final chance to justify her selection to the team. Turning her attention to the starting line, she watched as Bobbie took her mark. At that moment, she felt composed and confident they would win. "Wasn't this wonderful what was happening to me," she thought. "I was going to be a champion."

The starter's pistol fired and the runners sped away. From her vantage point, Jane felt that Bobbie was late off her mark, and assumed she didn't want to risk a false start. But Bobbie had always been a slow starter, not reaching her top speed right until the 50 meters mark. This was the case now, for Jane could see her gaining on the American, who was in front. As Bobbie came up to Ethel for the baton exchange, Jane held her breath. This was crucial, for it was all over if the first pass was missed. To her relief, it was clean.

She followed Ethel's progress down the back course, her clothing pressed against her body and her hair flying in the wind. As her teammate drew closer, Jane realized she was only moments from entering the race. She held her mark until Ethel was seven meters away, and then took off. Almost instantly, she could hear Ethel's spikes hitting the cinder track behind her, and felt the hard wood of the baton placed perfectly in her right hand. When the round stick hit her palm, Jane gripped it firmly, shifted gears, and accelerated quickly. She fixed her sight on the path ahead and set out, intent on running the fastest one hundred meters of her life. The fate of the relay team now rested on her legs.

"I had a feeling I was behind when I took the baton," she said, "but I didn't know for sure because the lanes were staggered." Whether it was the uncertainty of her position in the race or determination to run well, she moved like one possessed. As she rounded the final curve and rushed towards Myrtle, it appeared to Alex Gibb and others in the stands that the eighteen-year-old was trailing. But when Jane straightened out for the final handover, it was apparent that curves had suited the Toronto teenager just fine. The weak link on the relay team was in the lead by three yards and the Canadians were one hundred meters away from their first Olympic championship. Only a disaster could prevent it.

In a relay race, the baton must be passed within a twenty meters acceleration zone, or the team is disqualified. As soon as the incoming runner is seven to eight meters from the acceleration zone's starting line, the outgoing runner takes off at full speed, so no time is lost in the exchange. In Amsterdam, the girls had worked hard to perfect this skill. Now, in the final, Bobbie and Ethel had played their parts faultlessly. All that remained was for Jane and Myrtle to do the same.

As her teammates flashed around the track, Myrtle nervously marked their progress. The waiting affected her and, as the baton was passed from

Bobbie to Ethel to Jane, her anxiety mounted. Were they in first, second, or third place? Would the exchange between her and Jane be perfect? She needed to do well. It was important to make up for her earlier disaster and to dispel any doubts about her ability. But as Jane bore down on her, and in the lead, Myrtle's nerves got the better of her and she bolted. Approaching the acceleration zone, Jane was horrified to see Myrtle leave her mark too soon and at full speed. This was trouble enough, but Jane noticed that Myrtle was moving on the outside part of the lane, making it difficult for the exchange. Fighting to master these problems and avert disqualification, Jane knew time was running out, for she could see Myrtle drawing nearer to the end line of the acceleration zone and catastrophe.

"Our hearts were in our mouths," Ethel recalled, as she and Bobbie watched Jane struggle to reach Myrtle before it was too late. Smith uttered a fervent wish: "Jane will never catch you now, Myrtle, unless you slow up a bit." Yet, by an extraordinary effort, Jane got to Myrtle at the last possible moment. "I can remember seeing her foot come down [on the end line]," Jane said, "but by that time the baton was gone and she [Myrtle] was on her way." Watching this, Alex Gibb judged the exchange between them as "near a flop as anything could be." The one between the Americans, in second place, was perfect, and Elizabeth Robinson, the speedy winner of the 100 meters, was now in the race. Although Myrtle had a head start, Gibb agonized that the poor exchange by Jane and Myrtle might have hurt them. Had they opened the door for the Americans?

Myrtle Cook was grimly determined to show everyone she could run. Feeling the baton in her hand, and unaware of how close she had come to ruin, she set out, her eyes fixed on the tape one hundred meters away. Despite Elizabeth Robinson's effort, it wasn't enough on this day. Myrtle tore down the track and crossed the line in first place, in a time of $48\frac{2}{5}$ seconds. As one reporter put it: "Nothing could have withstood Myrtle's onslaught. It was her all." It was another world's record, breaking the one they had set the day before by a full second.

National Archives of Canada/PA150984

Myrtle Cook (right) crosses the finish line in first place, ahead of American Elizabeth Robinson, in the 4 x 100 meters relay final. For Cook, it was a happy finish to what had been, until then, a dismal Olympics.

Among the Canadians in the stands, there were smiles, tears, and gasps of relief. Hard luck and disappointment had dogged the women's team throughout the week. But, on the last day of competition, they had a first, and the Canadian flag was going to the masthead of the center flagpole. The applause in the stadium was deafening. They expected a great reception if they won, Gibb said, but they didn't anticipate the "wholehearted outburst" from the Dutch, whose relay team they had just defeated.

On the field, Bobbie, Ethel, and Jane ran towards a breathless Myrtle. Grabbing hold of her, the new Olympic champions laughed and whooped. Cameramen who were trying to get them to pose for pictures found it impossible: They were jumping up and down too much. Jane recalled thinking, "Well, it's over, we did it. Isn't that wonderful." The victory was particularly sweet for Myrtle. Since Tuesday, the heartbreak of the 100 meters had

National Archives of Canada/PA150984

The Canadian Olympic relay team following their victory: (left to right) Jane Bell, Myrtle Cook, Ethel Smith, and Bobbie Rosenfeld. They were so excited that the photographer had difficulty in getting them to stand still.

lingered – a painful reminder of what might have been. That was behind her now, and the despair of the past was lost in the joy of the present.

The results of the women's relay final appeared on the scoreboard and the loudspeakers blared throughout the stadium, "Champion d'Olympique, Premier – Canada." As 30,000 rose to their feet, the Canadian Red Ensign mounted the masthead while the band played "The Maple Leaf Forever." For Jane Bell, the injured member of the team, the scene was branded on her memory. "Of all the things that have happened in my life, many good things," she said, fifty years later, "I don't think I was ever as proud and as thrilled as when I stood and saw our flag going up and . . . the four of us with tears."

Following the anthem, the girls pulled on their sweat suits and joined the happy Canadians in the competitors' section. Unfortunately, the high spirits and exuberance that followed the performance of the women's relay team couldn't be sustained. Twenty minutes later, the men's 400 meters relay team was disqualified when Percy Williams and a teammate got mixed up in the exchange and dropped the baton. A better outcome occurred in the 1600 meters relay, where the Canadians finished third.

Despite the results in the men's relays, the performances of the Canadian athletes throughout the week were the talk of the nations present in Amsterdam. American observers, especially, were forced to make some painful admissions. "We are an outstanding nation in our achievements. But we are not a nation of supermen," a sportswriter for the *Los Angeles Examiner* said. In buttressing his comments, the writer referred to their defeats by Percy Williams, an unheard-of and unheralded Canadian youth. He also spoke of the shock provided by a handful of Canadian girls who had showed their heels to the American women in the relay. "This Canada nation needs a lot of watching," he said. Now, at the jumping pit in the stadium, another Canadian girl was poised to earn additional honors for the land of the Maple Leaf.

The high jump is an event in which the competitors are given three tries to clear a given height. If they fail, they are eliminated. Once the crossbar is raised, the successful candidates begin again. This continues until only one remains – the competitor who has jumped the highest and is the winner. Because of this format, the high-jump event is a contest of lengthy duration. The competition at the ninth Olympiad was no exception, lasting almost three hours.

The elimination trial in the women's running high jump began at two o'clock and continued during the relay races. When it finished, 19 of the 23 competitors had achieved the standard of 4 feet 6 inches, qualifying for the final. Among them was Ethel Catherwood. Her reputation as a high jumper was well known, but in Amsterdam it was her striking good looks that caught the public's fancy. Photographers and autograph seekers gathered whenever she appeared. Yet, as Jane Bell said, "Ethel did not like the celebrity status. She hated it when people bothered her." Eventually, it became too much. The constant requests forced her to retreat to the Pension Regina and remain there like a cloistered nun until the final day of competition.

To the other members of the women's team, she was a puzzle. Ethel Smith found her aloof and introverted. "You could not get too friendly with her," she said. "She was a quiet girl who never mixed very much." Jane, who was closer to Catherwood than anyone, admitted that she was a very private person. Nevertheless, she found her to be fun. On one occasion, the two of them filled the bathtub at the Pension Regina with cold water and gave Myrtle a dunking. But this was a side of Ethel few saw. During her stay in Amsterdam, she was a cool and distant enigma, spending much of her time alone at the boardinghouse, or with her sister, Ginger. The inseparability of

Canada's Sports Hall of Fame

Ethel Catherwood was surprised by the media frenzy that surrounded her.

the Catherwood sisters was such that Fred Marples, treasurer of the COC, dubbed them the "Siamese Twins."

The cold and damp of the day were unconducive to high-jumping, but the Canadians in the stadium were certain the Saskatoon Lily would do well. Yet, for the first time in her career, Ethel would be facing real competition. Among those expected to give her a battle were Marjorie Clark of South Africa and Holland's Carolina Gisolf, both of whom had jumped 5 feet 3 inches. Two American girls, Jean Shiley and Mildred Wiley, were considered lesser threats. As the afternoon wore on and her opponents were gradually eliminated, Ethel displayed the deft and unerring form that made her a winner. Sixteen-year-old Jean Shiley remembered the Canadian jumper: "I was an admirer of Ethel Catherwood. She was beautiful to look at and graceful over the bar." Shiley's opinion was shared by others. The judges of the event unanimously agreed that Ethel was the most agile and perfect jumper any of them had ever seen in action.

Because no Canadian officials were allowed on the field for the high-jump competition, and the other countries had at least two jumpers in the final, Ethel was all alone. This situation prompted a noble act of sportsman-ship by the Belgian competitors. During the 800 meters and the relay, the Canadians had shared a dressing room with the Belgian girls. As they had no one to look after them, Alex Gibb and Marie Parkes offered their services as masseuses. The generosity of the Canadian officials wasn't forgotten. When the three Belgian jumpers noticed that Ethel was by herself, they sat down beside her and, throughout the competition, they kept her company and took care of her. Following each of her jumps, they wrapped her up care-fully in her red Hudson's Bay blanket, removed her spikes, and cleaned them of mud and sand.

Ethel didn't take off her sweatpants until the bar was at 5 feet 1 inch. Her habit of never shedding her sweat suit until late in the competition was something Walter Knox had implanted. He understood the mental aspect of sport better than most, and knew the importance of a psychological edge for an athlete. Ethel acquired that advantage over her rivals, he felt, by leaving her warm-up outfit on for as long as possible in competition. "Just take your time," he always told her. "You know what you can do." When she made her first miss at 5 feet 1 inch, the Canadians had a scare and held their breath. Off came the sweatpants, but not the top, and she leapt easily over the bar on her second attempt.

During the competition, the partisan Dutch spectators were loud in support of their champion, Carolina Gisolf. Hopeful of victory as she jumped higher, they became louder with each successful attempt, amplifying the din, which filled the stadium. The American fans, who were conspicuous whenever their representatives competed, were almost as noisy. College yells resounded from where they sat, encouraging Mildred Wiley and Jean Shiley in their efforts. The outnumbered Canadian contingent did its best to match the volume of the opposition with shouts of "C-A-N-A-D-A, Catherwood, Catherwood, Catherwood." Sitting among them, an anxious Ginger Catherwood watched the contest, her apprehension increasing as the number of competitors dwindled. Each time Ethel jumped, she would cover her eyes, fearing the worst. Only when she heard the cheers of the Canadians around her would she remove her hands, knowing the jump was successful. And, as the afternoon wore on, the Saskatoon Lily continued to clear the bar. After three hours, only Wiley and Gisolf stood between her and high-jumping supremacy.

With the bar above 5 feet $1\frac{2}{5}$ inches, the three women prepared to tackle the new height. All were successful. The bar was raised to 5 feet 3 inches. This was unfamiliar territory for Wiley, but not the other two. All missed on their first attempt. And as the crossbar fell after each failed bid, a loud concerted sigh could be heard throughout the stadium. The crowd, hopeful of a better second effort, watched as the three tried once more. Again the American and the Dutch jumpers missed.

By now, Ethel had removed the sweatshirt she had worn throughout the competition. From every part of the stadium, attention focused on her second attempt. Those with binoculars trained them on the high-jump pit and the lone athlete in red shorts and white top. It was almost 4:45 P.M. when the tall dark-haired Canadian began her run towards the crossbar. In seconds, she reached her takeoff point. As she leapt into the air, a collective inhaling of breath could be heard from the 30,000 spectators. Using the scissors style, her right leg cleared the bar first. Then, a split second afterwards, her left leg followed. The roar in the stadium told her what she already knew: The jump was perfect.

The others realized they needed to do the same on their third and final attempt, or it was all over. Yet neither Wiley nor Gisolf could do it. In less than ten jumps, the Saskatoon Lily was the Olympic champion.

A sag in the bar revealed she had jumped 5 feet 2$\frac{9}{16}$ inches instead of 5 feet 3 inches, the height many thought to be the world's record. There was confusion about world records because of a misunderstanding between imperial and metric measures, poor communications, and a failure to register records. As a result, the standard of 5 feet 3 inches, which Ethel had jumped in Halifax, hadn't been recognized at the Olympics. Instead the officials used 5 feet 2½ inches, set the year before, as the world's mark for the women's high jump. Ethel's leap, therefore, was regarded as a world's record, and the *Official Guidebook of the Ninth Olympiad*, published afterwards by the Netherlands Olympic Committee, noted her achievement as such. Believing she had set the record, the high-jump officials didn't allow her to try a greater height.

It was unlikely she would have continued jumping, regardless. With all her challengers eliminated, the incentive to carry on was gone. Alex Gibb admitted that Ethel needed strong competition to bring out the best in her. Furthermore, after reaching 5 feet 2$\frac{9}{16}$ inches, Ethel lost heart. "She had already accomplished what she had left Canada to do," Gibb said, "and was not interested in anything but the championship." Ethel felt the same: "How much better can you get than first?"

But there was more. "She didn't have the passion for her sport the others did," Jane said. Bobbie Rosenfeld agreed. "Most of her ability was natural,"

Ethel Catherwood clears the bar at 5 feet 2⁹⁄₁₆ inches to win the women's high jump and the Canadian women's team's second championship of the afternoon.

National Archives of Canada / PA151016

Bobbie acknowledged, "and she did no great amount of training. Ethel's idea of a perfect day, as I found her at Amsterdam, was to lie abed with a box of rum-and-butter toffee and a ukelele, eating and strumming. The rum, the butter, and the toffee can split the credit for her performance in winning the Olympic high jump three ways."

Her final jump, identified as a world's record, produced a tremendous ovation from the throng that witnessed it. Her victory was received with more enthusiasm than any other Canadian achievement, except that of Percy Williams in the 100 meters. Ginger Catherwood, relieved the long ordeal was over and that it had ended happily, broke down completely. She wasn't alone. For the second time in the afternoon, P.J. Mulqueen watched the women triumph and shed tears of joy.

Down on the field, the new Olympic high-jump champion responded to the crowd's applause by bowing and blowing kisses. She displayed "the cool grace of a movie star," the *New York Times* correspondent remarked. Because Gisolf and Wiley were tied for second, a jump-off was necessary. So Ethel donned her sweat suit and joined the happy Canadians in the competitors' section to watch. She sat next to Percy Williams. During the visits of the men to the Pension Regina, the women were struck by how shy he was. "He wouldn't talk to the girls," Jane said. Yet Ethel made an effort to speak to him and a friendship developed. Now, in the exhilaration of the moment, she leaned over and kissed him. Some high-spirited Canadians grabbed them both, lifting the two athletes shoulder-high. The acclamation from the stands was repeated and Ethel waved her arms in response.

The jump-off ended with Gisolf's victory, and Ethel joined the partisan crowd in cheering the Dutch girl's success. Now that the second and third places were decided, her championship was announced over the loudspeakers and she made her way to the front of the stand. The band began "The Maple Leaf Forever," and the crowd rose from their seats. The Canadians, their hearts full, sang the anthem as loud as they could. The band was still off-key, but the attempt was better than the one following Percy's victory in the 100 meters. A year before, Ethel had confessed that her golden goal was a world's record to be credited to Canada. Standing as the world's champion in the Olympic Stadium, she had fulfilled that ambition. Everything she had ever wanted as an athlete was hers at that moment, and she was content.

The best the Canadians could do in the marathon was a tenth-place finish, yet the achievements of the Canadian women's team more than compensated. With two victories in two events, there was no denying that the day was, as one reporter expressed it, "an outstanding triumph for Canadian girlhood." Moreover, the Canadian women's team had earned a total of 34 points, enough to win the world's championship in track and field. The U.S. contingent and the German squad were second and third, with 28 and 23 points. The success of the Canadians was even more striking because they had entered one less event than the Americans and the Germans, who had competed and won points in all.

A proud Alex Gibb, reflecting on her team's performance, said, "With [34] . . . points to our credit, including two championships and the women's championship of the world, who will dare repeat the assertion made in Canada this spring that the girls would be excess baggage? Every girl on the team scored points for Canada." Against 121 athletes from 21 countries, whose total population was 300 million, a team of 6 from a country of less than 10 million had emerged victorious. Sportswriters were happy to give the women full measure for their feats. Under the title, "CANADA'S 'MATCHLESS SIX' CHAMPIONS," the *Globe*'s Mike Rodden said, "Canadian athletes won the world's championship as the ninth Olympiad neared its close at Amsterdam yesterday. The great victories achieved by Miss Ethel Catherwood of Saskatoon and the relay team, composed of Jane Bell, Fanny Rosenfeld, Ethel Smith, and Myrtle Cook, all of Toronto, won the title for their country." The Toronto *Evening Telegram*'s Tom Levine remarked, "All hail the conquering Canadian heroines! The best women athletes in the world! They lead all the women's teams at Amsterdam."

Bobbie Rosenfeld was singled out for her part in the team's success. She had competed every day, except one, running three times in the 100 meters, twice in the 800 meters, and twice in the sprint relay. Her second-place finish in the 100 meters, fifth in the 800 meters, and her part in the relay victory represented an amazing Olympic record. Of the 34 points earned by the Canadian women's team, "the wiry little 124-pound girl" played a role in 17 of them. Only Percy Williams' total of 20 points for the men's team was better. Nevertheless, Bobbie showed more versatility than any contestant at the Games, and was described as one of the "Iron Men" of the Canadian Olympic Team. The manager of the girls' team especially praised Bobbie's attitude. "All through the training period and in the hours of competition she displayed a rare spirit," Alex Gibb said, "that true competitive spirit which makes champions."

As the only individual winner of the women's squad, Ethel Catherwood received her share of media attention. The COC contemplated striking a medallion with engravings of her and Percy Williams on one side, and the Maple Leaf on the other. Hollywood was interested, and Ethel had received an offer to appear in films of the college sports type, wearing her Olympic costume.

The two victories achieved on the final day of track-and-field competition left everyone on the women's team euphoric. Their accomplishments and the world's athletic championship affirmed what they had believed all along: They were the best. Jane asked, "Where are our medals?" The others told her, "Don't worry, we're going to get them afterwards." Percy Williams arrived at the Pension Regina bearing huge boxes of candy to help the girls celebrate, and they were delighted by his gesture. He had a special present for Ethel Catherwood. It was a lace hanky, on which he had written, "We both come from the West."

Their competitions over, the girls were free from the rigors of training and curfews. Bobbie and some of the boys' team went to a small Dutch town to make merry. Their host kept tipping the orchestra leader to play "The Maple Leaf Forever." In one corner of the room, a group of Germans would come stiffly to attention with each playing.

After supper, Ethel Smith and Myrtle Cook met with a couple of Argonaut scullers and headed downtown. Because the rowers were still competing, they had to be in by ten o'clock and couldn't wander far. "This was one night we could really have fun," Ethel said, and neither she nor Myrtle wanted to go to bed early. They continued to the city center on their own. At a dance club, they met two members of the New Westminster Salmonbellies lacrosse team and partied until closing time. "So . . . [the boys] said, 'Let's take a hack back,'" Ethel recalled. "We went looking for a horse and buggy and found one. It was all good clean fun. None of this sexy stuff. Anyway we didn't go to bed that night."

When the youngest members of the team, Jane Bell and Jean Thompson, discovered they were on their own, they walked to the city's Dam Square in

Author's collection

Amsterdam's Dam Square, where Jane Bell and Jean Thompson went to look for other Canadians to celebrate their team's victories.

hopes of finding other Canadians with whom to celebrate. But after strolling around and wondering, "Where is everybody?", they returned to the Pension Regina. There was the chore of packing to be done, as they were leaving for Brussels early the next day. At two o'clock in the morning, they awoke to a commotion outside the boardinghouse. In the street, the Argonaut Eight scullers, Olympic rowing coach Joe Wright Senior's "pork and beaners," were gathered. To honor the women and their victories, they had come to serenade the team.

In the morning, the Canadian women said good-bye to Amsterdam and boarded the train at Centraal Station for Brussels. During the two and a half weeks they had been in the city, not all of the time was spent in Olympic competition. They had also been able to play the part of tourists, visiting places of interest and shopping for Dutch caps, windmill clocks, Delft plates, wooden shoes, and lace. Those who liked to walk had spent pleasant hours mingling with the Amsterdamers on the busy Nieuwendijk and the Kalverstraat, or hiking to Rembrandtplein, where a number of restaurants

National Archives of Canada/PA151005

The Argonaut Eight, from Toronto's Argonaut Rowing Club, following their loss to the United States in the semifinal of the eight-oared event on the Sloten Canal.

and cafes were located. Time had passed quickly and the girls were sorry to leave.

As the train moved out of the city into the countryside, the six members of the Canadian women's Olympic team gazed out the windows at the flat Dutch landscape of polders, dikes, and windmills. Each pondered the events of the past two and a half weeks. They knew something significant had happened in their lives, but, for now, it was impossible to assess the impact. Thoughts soon turned to family and friends in Canada.

Chapter Ten

Dr. Lamb's Bombshell

Olympic competition behind them, the Canadian women athletes were free to relax and enjoy the attractions of foreign capitals. In Brussels, they passed a pleasant afternoon touring a lace factory, purchasing souvenirs, and sightseeing. Boarding the train for Paris several hours later, they arrived that evening. The next day the group was up early and away by ten o'clock, happily anticipating a full day to explore the sights. Famous landmarks, such as the Eiffel Tower, Notre Dame, l'Arc de Triomphe, and the Palace of Versailles, beckoned.

In Amsterdam, meanwhile, the IAAF was convening on the second day of its congress at the Industrieele Club. President J.S. Edstrom began the session by reminding the delegates that at The Hague two years ago, they had decided that ladies' athletic events would be put on the program of the 1928 Olympic Games as a trial. The federation's executive council was pleased with the results and recommended that five or six events for women remain on the Olympic program. The congress now had to vote on this. Among those present were three representatives from Canada: Dr. A.S. Lamb, P.J. Mulqueen, and F.H. Marples. As president of the Amateur Athletic Union of Canada (AAU of C), Lamb would cast Canada's ballot. He recognized the importance of his vote, and three months before mailed copies of the federation's agenda to the AAU of C's Board of Governors, the secretaries of its branches and allied bodies, and all members of the COC. In an accompanying note, he asked for their comments. Of the one hundred letters he sent out, Lamb received not a single response.

In Amsterdam, he had brief conversations with Canadian officials about athletics for women at the Olympics. But wishing to go over the subject more thoroughly, Lamb called a meeting of the other members of the COC the night before the IAAF's vote on the matter. Pat Mulqueen and Fred Marples never appeared, although the others waited for some time. While the discussion he hoped for didn't occur, Lamb felt he had done everything he could to learn the feelings of the AAU of C and the COC. He would cast his vote according to his principles and the opinions he heard expressed by other Canadian officials in Amsterdam.

The debate among the delegates at the congress over women's athletics revealed a range of opinions. The Finnish delegate, who led the opposition, charged that athletic competitions for women were only a passing fad. Moreover, these sports didn't suit women. As one male doctor expressed it, even though women's limbs might be well developed, their hips and bust were impediments to the speed necessary for victory. The British representative, who was also opposed to women participating in the athletic part of the Olympic Games, conceded that Englishwomen might compete in the future if there was a full athletic program and a committee of women in charge of it. The Swiss delegate said he wasn't against female participation as such, but believed the ladies' events should be held on separate days from those of the men, or on a special day.

With equal fervor, the representatives from the United States, Greece, and Sweden spoke in favor of women athletes at the Olympics. The experiment at the ninth Olympiad was "a complete success," they contended, and women should continue to compete. Japan's delegate agreed. Feminine sport was steadily increasing in his country, he said, and the presence of women athletes at the Olympics would promote the trend.

Arthur Stanley Lamb was born in
Ballarat, Australia, in 1886. He trained
as a carpenter and continued his trade
after immigrating to Vancouver in
1907. Active in the local YMCA's
Leaders Corps, he went to the
International YMCA Training College
in Springfield, Massachusetts. As
many leading authorities in physical
education were qualified in medicine,
Lamb decided to become a doctor.
He attended McGill University's
School of Medicine and graduated
in 1917. After serving overseas, he
returned to McGill, where he
became the director of the
Department of Physical Education
when it was established in 1919-20.
In 1927, his hard work as secretary of
the Amateur Athletic Union of
Canada was recognized and he was
elected president of the organization.
A year later, he was chosen manager
of the Canadian Olympic Team.

Canadian Olympic Committee

At the federation's congress two years before, no woman had spoken on
the subject. In Amsterdam, however, three representatives from the *Fédération
Sportive Féminine Internationale* were invited to address the congress. In a
powerful speech, Lady Mary Heath of Great Britain said, "We are now your
comrades and co-workers in industry, commerce, art and science, why not in
athletics?" For Lady Heath, women's admission to the Olympics was more
than an equality issue. It was vital for the international development of feminine sport. "If you approve of athletics for women at all, you must approve
of participation in the Olympics," she said, "for women need the stimulus of
matching their prowess against others of the world's best athletes quite as
much as the men."

Despite her plea, the hard-liners were unbending. They raised the old quarrels, such as women weren't allowed in the ancient Greek Olympics, and that competitive sport was injurious to women's health. To the first contention, Lady Heath replied that the hop, step, and jump, fencing, and pistol-shooting weren't part of the original Olympics either, but this didn't stop them from being added to the modern Games. The examining physician of Berlin's women athletes addressed the second concern. In ten years of practise, he told the delegates, he found female athletes got married and had normal, healthy children just like nonathletes.

As he listened to the arguments from both sides, Dr. A.S. Lamb realized there was nothing new in them. Still, he wasn't a disinterested observer. The debate over women's participation in the Olympic Games represented for him the bigger issues of proper sports for women and who should control them. As a doctor and physical educator, he welcomed the growing interest and participation of girls and women in recreational activities following the First World War, but he also recognized that this new lifestyle was fraught with dangers. Play was a two-edged sword, he cautioned, and misdirected activities and emphasis might be harmful.

When he rose to address the IAAF congress, Dr. Lamb did so as the representative of the country whose six women athletes were the track-and-field champions of the world. The feat was impressive and the newspapers had made much of it. The victories of the relay quartette and Ethel Catherwood, and the stellar overall performance of Bobbie Rosenfeld were among the highlights of the athletic competition, and the Canadian girls were the talk of the Olympics. In view of this, Lamb was no minor figure at the congress: The delegates were much interested in what he had to say.

Speaking as one who had fifteen years' knowledge of feminine athletic sports, Lamb affirmed these sports were beneficial. Nevertheless, he was opposed to international athletic competitions for women and felt that such competitions shouldn't be on the Olympic program. With that, he sat down.

The brevity and content of his speech likely surprised many. Mulqueen asked him if the Canadian representatives at the IAAF congress had a right to express an opinion. Of this Dr. Lamb was certain: It was the AAU of C that was represented at the meeting, not the COC. As the Union's delegate, he had the authority to speak on its behalf. Furthermore, because neither Mulqueen nor Marples said anything and didn't disagree with his remarks, he assumed they shared his viewpoint.

The discussion over, President Edstrom put the question of ladies' events on the Olympic program to a vote. If doubts still lingered about his position, Lamb answered them by casting Canada's vote with Finland, Great Britain, Hungary, Italy, and Ireland against their continuance. Yet the stance of the powerful United States on the subject, and that of Greece – the birthplace of the ancient Olympics and site of the first modern one – decided the issue. Sixteen nations voted in favor of keeping women's athletic events. This meant that Canada would be recorded as the first winner of the women's track-and-field championship.

In voting the way he did, Dr. Lamb was consistent in his principles and beliefs. From the beginning, he questioned women's fitness for athletic contests as keen as those of the Olympics. "Physically and mentally, women are unsuited for meets of this nature," he said. "They are too highly strung and, no matter what their physical condition may be, they are bound to compete with so much at stake. Dire results often follow." How serious the injuries, he couldn't say, as women hadn't participated long enough, but there was another concern. Women's recent involvement meant they lacked men's sense of teamwork and the ability to be good losers. To develop these, Lamb said, women needed regulated and properly supervised games appropriate for their physical and mental growth. What were these games? They were tennis, badminton, swimming, skating, golf, and fencing. Track and field, therefore, was not the means, nor the Olympic Games the way. Rather than enhancing women's well-being, they threatened it.

Bobbie Rosenfeld and Myrtle Cook considered these theories nonsensical. Bobbie said she would gladly fall in line and support the opposition to women's track and field if given one case of a female athlete who suffered because of direct participation in athletics. Otherwise, she felt these ravings were "plain ordinary, everyday tommyrot." Myrtle declared that most who issued warnings, ultimatums, and the like had never raced in world competitions and therefore didn't know what effect they had physically. The critics were writing what they thought – not what they knew from experience.

Yet it was obvious to Lamb that certain events in Amsterdam widely supported his concerns. When the track-and-field program came to a close, he felt enormous relief. For him, the remarkable achievements of Canada's athletes in the Olympic Stadium against the world's best had been overshadowed by the uncontrolled and violent emotions of a few. The shameful conduct of Robinson and Mulqueen was depressing enough, but the disqualification of Myrtle Cook and the sight of her standing at the side of the track, tears streaming down her face, confirmed his worst fears. And when the protest occurred after the race, it only added to his woes. Not only was the principle of good sportsmanship violated, but a dubious message was conveyed to the girls' team.

The protest upset him because he saw in it the menace facing Canadian sportswomen. The win-at-all-costs mentality smacked of professionalism, a problem affecting men's sports. Led as it was by Mulqueen and Robinson, the outcry over the result of the women's 100 meters final showed Lamb what could happen to women's sports with men in control. They were in peril of being hijacked by unscrupulous promoters and others for self-glorification and financial gain. Only a policy of women's athletics being governed by women would prevent this, Lamb believed. But as long as they were part of the Olympics where men were in charge, it was impossible.

The low point came two days later, in the women's 800 meters. The sportsmanship of Bobbie Rosenfeld was praiseworthy, but it was the only bright spot in an event marked by controversy. The flap created by Mulqueen and Robinson over the pacing of an American by a teammate, and the sharp words of Mulqueen to the IAAF president about the incident were sufficiently distressing. But it was the scene of exhausted women on the infield at the end of the final and a prostrate Jean Thompson, sobbing uncontrollably in Bobbie Rosenfeld's arms, that most affected Lamb. For him, the sad spectacle was indisputable proof that women were physically and mentally unsuited for meets as demanding as the Olympic Games. Furthermore, the reaction of Thompson to her fourth-place finish and of Cook to her disqualification showed that women lacked the "good losing" qualities necessary to compete.

In casting his vote against women's future participation, Dr. Lamb was convinced he had faithfully represented the position of the AAU of C. He was certain the others in Amsterdam felt the same. "On no occasion did I hear anyone, who might be considered as a Canadian official, favor a continuance of the present policy," he said, "but, on the other hand, there were many outspoken opinions against it." In this, he was mistaken. If he had spoken to Alex Gibb, or discussed the matter more closely with Bobby Robinson, he would have discovered at least two Canadian officials who thought differently.

When Lamb called the special conference the evening before the vote to discuss women's athletics at the Olympics, Robinson had already left Amsterdam for a motor tour of the battlefields of France. Had he been at the meeting, he would have denied that women's participation at the Olympic Games was undesirable. What he did say, however, was that it was undesirable to hold their events at the same time as the men's. He thought that separate days or separate programs would be better, but that the innovation of girls' athletics at the Olympics was a success.

Alex Gibb was in London with the women's team when she learned of Lamb's vote. Stunned and humiliated, she told curious English reporters, "He evidently thinks so little of what our sextette did against worldwide competition that he voted against Canada or any other nation being permitted to have women participate at future Olympic Games." Seldom, if ever, did he consult with those directly involved, she charged, and even though she was manager of the girls' team and Canada's representative on the *Fédération Sportive Féminine Internationale*, he never conferred with her.

In an attempt to explain Lamb's "strange vote," Gibb attributed it to geography. He was from Montreal, she said, where competitive athletics for women were practically "a minus quantity." Moreover, the biggest city of Canada never had an outstanding female athlete, nor did it have a single representative at the final Olympic Trials in Halifax. Undoubtedly, this was due to the objection that existed in Montreal against competitive sport for women. Whatever Lamb's reasons, Gibb vowed the Women's Amateur Athletic Federation in Canada would never accept a vote of this kind without knowing if it was a personal vote or a Canadian one. For Alex Gibb, the answer was already clear: "Dr. Lamb abrogated to himself the complete right to decide all Olympic issues."

Lamb's action was seen as one more act in the Olympic melodrama involving Canadians. As a reluctant participant in the farce, Dr. Lamb lamented the effect it had on everyone. He confessed that Canada had achieved two records at Amsterdam: first, the marvelous results of her athletes; and second, the most deplorable reports of misunderstandings, strife, discord, and bad feeling, which were sent back home.

Unfortunately, the nonsense would continue. Sportswriter Mike Rodden of the *Globe* predicted a final explosion of such magnitude that the incidents that preceded it would pale in comparison. "Protests, counter protests, and protests against protests marred Canada's participation in the 1928 Olympiad, and there will be a reaction and a showdown," he said. "Dr. Lamb hurled a bombshell with telling effect when he voted against having women compete in the world's championship events. It is alleged that he consulted no one, and this despite the fact that the Canadian women's team won the title."

Chapter Eleven

A Homecoming like No Other

The downpour that began the night before continued into the early morning of August 25, 1928, as the SS *Laurentic*, carrying the Canadian women's athletic team, part of the men's rowing team, and the advance guard of the men's track-and-field athletes from the Amsterdam Olympics, sailed into the port of Quebec City. Noises from the ship docking roused the women and, by six o'clock, they were out of bed, dressed, and on deck for their first view of home. Hopeful of sunshine, they discovered instead a cold and rainy day. This cast a pall over everyone, but within an hour the skies cleared. The promise of fine weather and the cheers from the stevedores unloading the *Laurentic*'s cargo lifted their spirits. And when the official delegation from the Toronto and the Ontario governments arrived on board, offering congratulations and promising a reception in the Queen City second to none, the girls felt much better.

They had been gone since the middle of July and were homesick. Still, it had been an unforgettable adventure. Traveling on an ocean liner; competing at an Olympic Games; visiting Brussels, London, and Paris; and riding in an airplane after the Olympics, from London to Paris and back, had given them a lifetime of memories. They were returning with souvenirs: wooden shoes from Holland, lace from Belgium, and clothes from

England. They had descended on the stores "with the enthusiasm of an art collector," one reporter said. As proof of their shopping ardor, the women were bringing back thirty-five pieces of luggage. They had left Canada with twenty-five. But they were tired of touring, shopping, and competing: They longed to be home.

The stopover in Quebec City was brief, and the ship was soon steaming upriver on the final leg of its journey. It was an opportunity for the girls to finish packing, pose for pictures, and look at the sights along the St. Lawrence. When the *Laurentic* arrived in Montreal at ten o'clock that evening, they were relieved their travels were almost over. As the brilliantly lit vessel made its way around the bend into the city's harbor, those on deck were startled by the sight of hundreds of people crowding the wharf and harbor sheds. The papers had announced the team's arrival time and many had come to see the fun. While the boat docked, the large and noisy throng burst forth, shouting greetings and congratulations to the returning Olympians.

The reception was so unexpected and the numbers so daunting that Ethel Catherwood drew back from the boat's rail in alarm. But, pushed from behind by her teammates, she was soon smiling and waving in response. The girls, dressed in their Olympic uniforms, were easily spotted, illuminated by the lights from the harbor sheds. Many Torontonians had made the trip to Montreal and, as they recognized a member of the team, they called out to them by name. Mayor Camillien Houde was on the dock to extend an official welcome. As the Olympic party came ashore, each member was introduced to the mayor, whose lively personality and banter appealed to the athletes.

Celebrities they might be, but they weren't exempt from passing through customs. The only one to suffer from the regulations was Myrtle Cook: An officer demanded she pay duty on a large and furry toy dog she had purchased on the boat. Once they were processed, the women found themselves surrounded by the crowd and questioned by newspapermen. Myrtle denied that she was going to be married, and Ethel Catherwood refuted stories about a career in motion pictures. Ethel Smith said she was giving up athletics after her marriage in the fall. Bobbie was asked about the controversial finish in the women's race. "If I had won that 100 meters race I'd have got a synagogue," she joked. "I won't even get a pew now." Jean said she was returning to Penetang High School to finish her education, and Jane told newsmen she was entering Toronto's Margaret Eaton School of Physical Education in September to become a physical education teacher.

The celebration on the docks continued for over two hours. The women posed for photographers, answered questions, and acknowledged the crowd's good wishes. Ever since Amsterdam, there had been one question on everyone's mind: "Don't you think the folks at home will be glad we won?" The answer was found on the smiling faces and acclamation from everyone who welcomed them. If additional proof was needed of Canada's pride, it was found in numerous articles that appeared throughout the country. One in the Toronto *Evening Telegram* entitled, "CANADIAN GIRLS WONDERFUL WIN WORLD CHAMPIONSHIPS," was typical. "The feat of these girls is nothing short of marvellous," the writer said. "They won glory, fame, and honor for their native home and land and for themselves."

"HOME TO TORONTO is the slogan now," Alex Gibb announced, on the morning of Monday, August 27. The tributes in Montreal were gratifying, but thoughts turned to Toronto and the welcome celebrations there. The women knew they would have to make a speech and each member of the team spent time writing her own. "I knew mine backwards first," Jane said. As they traveled westward by train, they discovered all along the route – at Brockville, Gananoque Junction, Napanee, Belleville, Cobourg, Port Hope, and Oshawa – crowds were waiting. At each stop, people surged forward, surrounded the cars, and shook the hands of anybody connected with the team. They knew them all – Ethel Catherwood, the girls' relay team, and Jean Thompson.

The Canadian Olympians arrived at Union Station about seven o'clock, and there were 200,000 people waiting to greet them. As the women exited the train, carrying stuffed bears, dolls, and bunnies from overseas, they were met by cheers, handshakes, and hats thrown into the air. Parents fought

City of Toronto Archives, Fonds 1266, Item 14500

Members of the women's Olympic team wait for the parade to start: (left to right) Marie Parkes, Dorothy Prior, Jean Thompson, and Jane Bell. Olympic rower Jack Guest (in dark suit) is sitting in front of Parkes.

City of Toronto Archives, Fonds 1266, Item 14496

In another car, (left to right) Ethel Catherwood, Bobbie Rosenfeld, Ethel Smith, Alex Gibb, and Myrtle Cook (not shown) await the procession.

through the crowd to embrace their offspring, and one woman was said to have kissed a member of the girls' team a hundred times. Nobody kissed Ethel Catherwood, although many would have liked to. When they reached the station's main rotunda, the band of the Queen's Own Rifles struck up "See the Conquering Hero Comes," followed by "The Maple Leaf Forever." The group filed out to Front Street to the strains of "Colonel Bogey." Here the real welcome began. The multitude cheered and hollered; the girls kissed their friends or relatives; the boys shouted a casual "hello-there" to cover their deeper emotions of being back home.

The procession, a mile in length, was led by the carriage of the National Ladies' Club, drawn by a team of nine spirited gray horses. The guests of honor rode in three open cars, sitting high on top of the seats. There was no point along the four mile route that didn't have its cheering throngs and honking autos. On Bay Street, confetti rained down on the athletes. At University Avenue, buglers from the armories added to the continuous cacophony of noise and, at the Cowan Avenue fire station, the firemen rang the bells to greet them as they passed. Cheers and shouts of "Hurrah!" "Hello, Fanny," "Hello, Jean," "Good girl, Ethel!" were directed at members of the women's team. Jane was surprised to see her younger brother wearing long white flannel pants. When she left, he was a little boy in shorts, but now he was grown up.

For Bobbie, the parade was her kind of event. It seemed that she knew every second person along the route, every policeman, and all the firemen, too. Living up to her reputation, she had a different answer for every cheer. When the parade reached the Patterson Chocolate Company, her place of work on Queen Street, she saw fellow employees whooping from the windows and waving large white-and-green streamers in her honor. For one of the few times in her life, Bobbie was speechless. Somebody from Patterson's ran out and presented the women with boxes of chocolates, which they proceeded to throw at the boys running alongside their cars, the pressmen behind, and the mounted police. Ginger Catherwood, unhappy with the snail's pace of the procession, complained she never expected to ride so

City of Toronto Archives, Fonds 1266, Item 14503

A special float dedicated to Bobbie Rosenfeld passes by in the parade. On it are some of Bobbie's teammates from the Pats softball team and the Lakesides basketball team.

slowly again, unless it was at her own funeral. Bobbie replied that as far as she was concerned, they could go on traveling slowly forever.

The parade reached Sunnyside at nine o'clock. A crowd of 100,000 had been waiting since six o'clock to greet them. When the athletes appeared, the multitude quickly forgot its impatience and pushed forward to obtain a better view. The crush was so intense that the guests of honor struggled to make it to the platform, and a few of the less rugged on the welcoming committee never made it at all. As they lined up on the stage, they were greeted by Mayor McBride and Ontario Premier G. Howard Ferguson. Below, the bands accompanied the crowd as it sang, "The Gang's All Here," "She's A Jolly Good Fellow," and "She's A Daisy Just Now." To show their appreciation,

City of Toronto Archives, Fonds 1266, Item 14492

In front of Toronto's Union Station, Joe Wright Jr. waves to the crowd waiting to welcome him home. Standing beside him is Mayor Sam McBride.

the women athletes, led by Bobbie, gave the yell of the Olympic team: "Canada, Canada, C-A-N-A-D-A, Canada."

Mayor McBride began the program. They were assembled tonight to add one more glorious chapter to Toronto's enviable sporting history, he said. He introduced Joe Wright Jr. and presented him with a set of silver flatware on behalf of the city. The girls' Olympic relay team was next and each member was given a silver tea service. When Bobbie's name was called, the crowd went wild.

The mayor began, "Miss Fanny Rosenfeld is Canada's champion all-round lady athlete."

"We know it," responded the crowd.

And when McBride referred to Bobbie's second-place finish in the 100 meter race, the multitude shouted, "First!", expressing their opinion about the questionable finish.

Bobbie replied that it was a thrill to make the team and travel to Amsterdam, but it was a bigger thrill returning home. "We wanted to see our flag go to the top," she told the crowd. "I leave it to you whether it did or whether it did not."

For Jane, who knew her speech so well, the moment was an embarrassing one. "I opened my mouth and there was nothing," she said. "The more I tried, the harder it was, and the silence got more and more uncomfortable." Finally, the mayor came to her rescue.

"Well, this speaks for itself," he remarked. "It's obvious that Jane is so glad to be home that she's speechless." Mrs. Bell couldn't believe it. Her daughter, who was never at a loss for words, was tongue-tied.

The presentation to Ethel Catherwood was a popular one and the crowd's applause proved it. Toronto had adopted the Saskatoon Lily as its own and was happy to welcome its hero home. "I was only too glad to be able to win because it was for Canada," she said.

Jean Thompson, the Penetanguishene Pansy, accepted a wristwatch as a token of the city's esteem, and responded, "I didn't do what I wanted to do. I'm very sorry, but I'm glad to get a few points for Canada." Her apology was unnecessary because she had tried her best and everybody knew it. As the crowd swelled around the platform party afterwards, attempting to shake their hands, the pride felt was not for any one member, but for the team as a whole.

The celebration moved on to Withrow Park, where another reception, arranged by the West Danforth Business Men's Association, awaited them. Mounted police and motorcycle officers sped them on their way, stopping traffic at intersections and holding up streetcars so they could pass without interruption. At the park, 10,000 east enders were waiting to salute the Olympic athletes. The reception was scheduled to begin at nine o'clock, but the guests of honor didn't arrive until almost eleven. Yet the long delay seemed to improve the crowd's spirits and, when the Olympians finally appeared, the throng lost all reserve and broke into a vocal barrage.

Again there were presentations – a mantel clock for Joe Wright Jr. and sequined purses and bouquets of flowers for the women – and once more, there were speeches of appreciation. For Ethel Smith, however, there remained one final party. Arriving home about midnight, she found her neighbors waiting. The street was alight with lanterns and bright with flags to welcome their famous daughter.

For Ethel and the others, it had been a busy and exhausting day, and they were weary. It was a homecoming like no other – an outpouring of emotion so great and so generous that the girls were overwhelmed. Alex Gibb spoke for them all when she said, "The people of Toronto will never know how much it meant to come home and be welcomed in so wholehearted a manner." That night when they collapsed into bed, their heads spinning from the excitement and activity of the past forty-eight hours, they felt they could sleep forever.

Jean Thompson returned to Penetang on the evening of August 29, and was given the greatest reception in the small town's history. The scene at the railway station was lit by torches: old brooms soaked in coal oil, carried by older boys. Among the crowd, a number held bouquets of pansies in honor of their Penetang Pansy. As the train came in, the crowd let loose with cheer after cheer. These became a roar when Jean appeared in her Olympic uniform. After a short speech of welcome, the mayor escorted her to a waiting car. A spontaneous parade formed, consisting of the guest of honor, the town band, the torchbearers, and the throng who was there to see her. It made its way up Main Street to the cenotaph, where a gaily decorated fire engine served as an improvised platform.

In response to the address of welcome, Jean expressed her gratitude for the love of her friends. Her world fame, she said, was due to the encouragement given her by those in her hometown. The mayor gave a short speech and presented her with an octagonal silver cup. Following a few comments from others, selections from the band, and the national anthem, the reception came to an end. She was surrounded by friends, who shook her hand and embraced her, some wiping away tears of joy.

Six days after the big Toronto reception, Ethel Catherwood and her sister, Ginger, boarded the Canadian National Railways train at Union Station for Saskatoon. It had been eight months since they had left, and they were looking forward to coming home for an extended visit. Although she now lived in Toronto, Ethel's heart was still in Saskatoon. At Montreal, en route to the Olympics, a reporter called her a "Toronto product," and she took exception to it. She was from Saskatoon, Saskatchewan, she told him, and was proud of it. The Hub City was equally proud of its native daughter, for she had accomplished great things. "Our Ethel" was Saskatoon's first world titleholder and its citizens were eager to greet their conquering hero.

In Saskatoon, people began arriving at the railway station sometime before noon and, by lunch hour, a crowd of 2,000 jammed every available space on the platform. Excitement like this hadn't been seen since Armistice Day in 1918. Students, both past and present, from Ethel's old school, Bedford Road

Photo #PH 88-604 by Gibson Photos, courtesy of the Saskatoon Public Library – Local History Room

Ethel Catherwood's old high school, Bedford Road Collegiate, was proud of its Olympic high-jump champion and held a special ceremony to honor its famous graduate. Ethel, wearing her Olympic uniform, is seated at the left, in front of the Union Jack flag.

Collegiate, were there in full force, shouting the school cry and adding to the noise and confusion. The crowd was so large that Mrs. Catherwood needed persuading to leave the car and join her husband and children on the plat-form. When the Continental Limited pulled into the station at 12:20 P.M., a mad, scrambling, shouting mob was waiting. As the Saskatoon Lily appeared on the train car's steps in her Olympic uniform, there was a shout of, "There she is," and the throng rushed towards her, eager to shake her hand.

Saskatoon proclaimed "Ethel Catherwood Day" on September 26. In her honor, the afternoon was declared a public holiday. A parade, consisting of a motorcade, bands, and students from the city's three high schools, began from city hall and ended at City Park, where a formal reception took place. Ethel was presented with a $3,000 trust fund, which she would use to study piano at the Toronto Conservatory of Music. In his address, the mayor said that Ethel was an example of what could be done by determination and persist-ent training. She showed there were no shortcuts to success. He acknowl-edged the assistance she had received along the way, especially that of Joe Griffiths, whose coaching played a large part in her success at Amsterdam. In a brief reply, Ethel offered her thanks for the reception and trust fund, adding that she was happy to bring the championship to Saskatoon.

In Toronto, delight in Bobbie Rosenfeld's Olympic accomplishments ran high among the city's Jewish community. A committee was formed and sub-scriptions collected to purchase an automobile to honor the most versatile female athlete in Canada. At an afternoon tea held in the King Edward Hotel and attended by over a hundred friends, Bobbie was presented with a maroon-colored Durant sports coupe, a 10,000-mile service contract, and a supply of gasoline. The gift was the highlight of the afternoon, but the Junior Council of Jewish Women also showed their appreciation with a jeweled perfume tray and a trinket box.

★

Author's collection

In the months following the Olympics, Bobbie Rosenfeld quickly resumed her busy sports career, playing basketball, hockey, and training for the Millrose Games.

A party of a different kind awaited Dr. A.S. Lamb at the annual meeting of the AAU of C at Port Arthur, Ontario, in December. In a stormy and rancorous session, the Olympic dirty laundry was aired once more as each side defended its actions and attacked the other. One delegate remarked, "We get 'roasted' Lamb downstairs and fried lamb chops upstairs." When the smoke from the "Battle of Port Arthur" cleared, Dr. Lamb had resigned as president of the AAU of C and secretary of the COC. It would be four years before he attended another meeting of the Athletic Union.

For Gibb, Mulqueen, and Robinson, the defeat of Dr. Lamb was a satisfying end to the Olympic unpleasantness. Not only was it a vindication of their actions at Amsterdam, but it affirmed their stand that female athletes belonged at the Olympic Games. The fight, however, was far from over. It continued into the next decade, forcing spokeswomen such as Alex Gibb, Phyllis Griffiths, Myrtle Cook, and Bobbie Rosenfeld time and again to defend the right of women to participate in sport and to compete at the Olympics.

By the end of the year, the members of the girls' team resumed their interrupted lives. Jean Thompson was attending Penetang High School. Teddy Oke announced she was moving to Toronto in January to join his Parkdale Ladies' Athletic Club and to complete a business course. She would then work in his brokerage firm. Another Parkdale member, Jane Bell, was enrolled at the Margaret Eaton School of Physical Education. In October, Ethel Smith married, and the members of the women's team, except Ethel Catherwood, who was in Saskatoon, attended. Bobbie Rosenfeld, now a sales representative at Patterson Chocolates, returned to her life of hockey and basketball. Myrtle Cook was coaching the Canadian Ladies' track athletes once more and training hard in her spare time, hopeful of an opportunity to compete against Elizabeth Robinson. Ethel Catherwood was at the Royal Conservatory of Music in Toronto, studying piano, and completing her business course at Shaw's.

It was difficult for the six to pick up where they left off because of their Olympic achievements. "In 1928, the Canadian women's team blasted the scene," Munroe Bourne, a member of the Canadian Olympic swim squad, said years later. "They were really the dominant team [at the Olympics]." As the first world champions in women's athletics, they were international celebrities, and Canada was proud of what they had accomplished. For most of the 1920s, Canadians had exalted American sports heroes, but the Amsterdam Olympics changed that. In Percy Williams and the "Matchless Six," the country had heroes of its own. "They are a credit to Canada on and off the field," Lou Marsh said, "an advertisement the country could not buy if the government spent its entire budget."

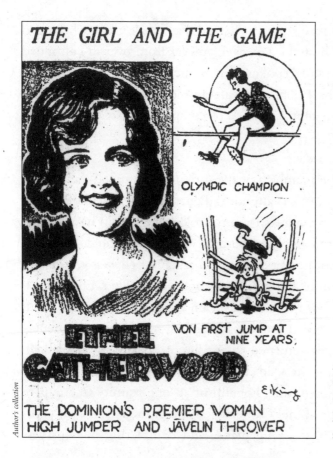

Author's collection

As the only individual Olympic champion on the Canadian women's team, Ethel Catherwood gained special renown.

The publicity and honors bestowed on Canada's female Olympians didn't go unnoticed by the nation's girl athletes. Alex Gibb remarked that since returning home, she found Toronto school yards crowded with young girls anxious to be future Bobbie Rosenfelds and Ethel Catherwoods. The boost given women's athletics, however, was felt far beyond the Queen City. Throughout the country, the example of the first women's team inspired others and encouraged their dreams that, someday, they too might represent Canada at an Olympic Games. Four years later, when it was time to select the women's squad for another Olympiad, the nine athletes chosen came from all parts of the country.

Chapter Twelve

Changed Lives

The memory of the big reception in Toronto, which Lou Marsh described as "the greatest ever accorded to a winning athlete or set of athletes in the city," stayed with Canada's first female summer Olympians all of their lives. "Yes, it was marvelous," Myrtle remembered. "And that's when I decided that wasn't the end and I was going to stay in competition as long as I could, and that when finished I would try and train other girls." Ethel Smith remarked, "I thought it was so wonderful. They treated us very well when we got back." Jane said, "We were the toast of the town. I thought it was great being a celebrity." Bobbie also recalled the acknowledgment they received when they returned: "We were on everybody's tongue," she said.

But, with the passage of time, perspectives changed. As the events in Amsterdam became part of a larger personal history, each woman reconstructed her impression of that period. For Jane, the response to her Olympic achievement remained a puzzle for much of her life. "I never really thought I did anything that anyone should make a fuss about," she reckoned. "I was very fortunate to be in the right place at the right time doing what I wanted to do." Myrtle always wondered about the missed opportunity, about what might have been. "I still dream about it," she said, many years later. "It's something you have to live with the rest of your life." Jean also carried her Olympic disappointment, but was able to put the memory of it behind her. For Bobbie, the Olympics became a highlight of an outstanding athletic career. Ethel Smith looked back on that splendid summer of 1928 and wished she could live it once more. Yet the one who possessed the brightest chance for a fairytale life after the Olympics became resentful and reclusive. Ethel Catherwood gave away all her trophies and medals and refused to discuss her Olympic experience, happy to let it slip into obscurity.

By the end of the year, after the celebrations were over, Bobbie Rosenfeld resumed her hectic schedule of sports. In January, she was involved in basketball, hockey, and bowling, as well as training with the relay team for the Millrose Games in New York City. Phyllis Griffiths, amazed at Rosenfeld's timetable, remarked that very few women, or men for that matter, could stand such a strenuous program. She was the backbone of the defense of the Lakeside basketball team, the center of the Pats hockey squad, and the lead runner for the Olympic relay team. Alex Gibb felt all this exertion was harmful, and feared it would affect Bobbie's performance at the Millrose Games.

The big meet at Madison Square Garden presented the opportunity to settle an old score when it was learned that Elizabeth Robinson, the winner of the Olympic 100 meters, would lead off for the American relay squad. She and Bobbie Rosenfeld would face each other for the first time since Amsterdam. This was the chance to prove once and for all who was the best female sprinter in the world. But Alex Gibb's worries were justified. Bobbie was worn out from her rigorous schedule. A week before she had been knocked unconscious in a hockey game, when smacked over the head with a hockey stick. She was in no shape for the race, but her teammates believed her courage and grit would carry her through.

After the first leg of the relay, there was no doubt about the winner. "Bobby [Bobbie] just trimmed Betty [Elizabeth] five nice luscious yards in the hundred and ten," Lou Marsh gloated. "And she beat her at every point in the race." With a good lead by Bobbie, the Canadian team seemed certain of victory, until Myrtle caused a mix-up on the exchange from Jane and dropped the baton. The mistake cost them the race and left everyone fuming at Myrtle. An unhappy finish, but Bobbie had taken her revenge. After completing her part of the relay, she ran over to P.J. Mulqueen, who was watching, and said, "Now, maybe I will get that synagogue." Still, she realized it wasn't the same as winning at the Olympics.

On her return from New York, Bobbie announced her retirement from track and field: "I'm not like the brook, you know. I can't go on forever." She was tired of running and wanted to concentrate on basketball, hockey, and softball, the sports she truly loved. Another Olympic Games wasn't in her future, and she joked that if she went, it would be as the water boy. She would be missed, and her remarkable record in athletics at the time stood as a testament to her outstanding ability. She was the Canadian record holder in the standing broad jump, eight pound shot put, the running broad jump, and the discus. Although she would no longer be a participant, Bobbie would remain involved with athletics. Her club had a number of junior sprinters and she would be coaching them.

In September 1929, Bobbie was struck down by rheumatoid arthritis. It was so sudden and severe that the doctor advised her right foot be amputated. The prospect of being forever removed from the life she loved was unthinkable. "What was I supposed to do, become an invalid?" she asked. Enduring months of painful recuperation, Bobbie eventually returned to her busy sports routine and was again one of the best. In February 1935, however, after a month of feeling unwell, she went to see her doctor, who diagnosed a double hernia. An operation to repair the ruptures was successful and everyone expected her return to competitive sports. But when Alex Gibb visited her in the hospital more than a week after the operation, she found a depressed Bobbie Rosenfeld. "All this about my being back in softball and basketball in a couple of months is just hooey," she declared, giving her pillow a decisive poke. "I am on the sidelines of sport for good. You can write in your column I am going in for coaching and managing some of these softball and basketball teams instead of being a player."

For Myrtle Cook, the sad news meant the last of the "Matchless Six" was calling it a day. Of all of them, Bobbie was the one who played the longest and the hardest. Still, Myrtle knew her old teammate well and the important role sport played in her life. "She loves the game . . . all games . . . too much to pass entirely out of the picture," Myrtle said. Over the next two years, Bobbie was never far from the sports scene, as president of the Ladies' Ontario Hockey Association, coach of the Toronto Pals girls' hockey team, and manager of the Lakeside Ladies softball team.

In April 1937, articles about women's sports written by Bobbie Rosenfeld began appearing in the Toronto *Globe and Mail*. The *Telegram*'s Phyllis Griffiths and the *Star*'s Alex Gibb had been writing about feminine sport since 1928. The *Globe* decided it was time to do the same and hired the country's most outstanding woman athlete. In December, a regular column, eventually called SPORTS REEL, with her byline began.

During the eighteen and a half years the column ran, Bobbie provided her outspoken views on a variety of sports topics. A favorite subject was the Olympic Games. As Canadian Olympic performances in track and field declined after 1928, she suggested the government provide support to schools and universities for athletic purposes. She also proposed a countrywide training program in order to discover Olympic candidates and the appointment of a full-time national coach. Her comments weren't always appreciated. When she accused Canadian athletes "of seeking channels of excuse and escape" for their poor showing at the 1948 London Olympics – their only medal being a bronze in the women's 4 x 100 meters relay – a reader called her a communist.

Despite the passage of time, Bobbie continued to be recognized for her achievements in sport. In December 1950, Canadian sportswriters and radio broadcasters voted her Canada's outstanding all-round woman athlete of the last fifty years. She considered the honor "her biggest victory," yet she never forgot her experience at the 1928 Olympics. Prior to the Rome Olympics in

Canada's Sports Hall of Fame

An older Bobbie Rosenfeld looks at a picture of her younger self at Canada's Sports Hall of Fame. She, Ethel Smith, Myrtle Cook, Jane Bell, and Ethel Catherwood were among the Hall's first inductees in 1955.

1960, she told an interviewer, "If [Canadian athletes] . . . enjoy Olympic competition the way I did, they'll come back just as enthusiastic about being at an Olympic Games for Canada."

When Bobbie retired from the *Globe and Mail* in 1966, she was asked by a reporter to name the most interesting personality she had met during her newspaper career. "I was a character in a way," she replied, and she was. But if ever there was a single athlete who defined the "golden age of sports" for Canadian women during the interwar period, she was that person. And if ever there was a single event that marked the high point of women's sports, it was the 1928 Olympic Games. For Bobbie, the episode remained an important part of an athletic career filled with notable achievements. "The thrill of being at the Olympics for Canada at Amsterdam in '28 is indelibly stamped in my mind," she said. "I don't think I'll every forget the emotional pitch of all the excitement, the crowds cheering, the teams parading behind the various banners, and the Royal salute from the box. I think those things never leave you."

Bobbie died in 1969, but she continues to be linked with sportswomen who have achieved international recognition. Annually, the Canadian female athlete of the year is presented with the Bobbie Rosenfeld Award, chosen by the country's sportswriters and sports broadcasters.

In January 1929, Jean Thompson came to Toronto and joined Teddy Oke's Parkdale Ladies' Athletic Club. As promised, Oke sent Jean to business school and gave her a job in his brokerage firm. She remained active in sports, playing basketball and softball for Parkdale and competing as a member of its athletic team. At the Ontario Championships that summer, she won the shot put, the discus throw, and the running broad jump. "This young star bids high for the place held by Fanny Rosenfeld as Canada's most versatile athlete," one sportswriter said. Yet the motivation to participate in another Olympics was gone and her specialty, the 800 meters, was no longer part of the Games. It had been removed after Amsterdam.

In her later years, married and living in Ste. Anne-de-Bellevue, Quebec, Jean never spoke much about her athletic achievements or the Olympic Games. She never thought they were a big thing. Her family felt otherwise, and stories of her accomplishments were passed from one generation to the next. In 1975, she received national recognition of sorts when a book about Canadian winners at the Summer Olympics was published. A picture of her winning the 800 meters heat in Amsterdam appeared on the cover.

Penetanguishene remembered the seventeen-year-old who had brought honor to the town in 1928 as the Penetang Pansy, and elected her to its Sports Hall Of Fame. In 1967, Jean was invited back as part of Penetanguishene's centennial celebrations. At the Sportsmen's Dinner, a speaker mentioned the 800 meters race at the Amsterdam Olympics, but for Jean it was ancient history. Her love of sports, however, remained until she died in 1976. She

Jean Thompson (left) and her sister-in-law in the early 1970s.

Brenda Hawes

was a good golfer, curler, and badminton player. An inspiration to the family, she often said that if the desire was great, then anything was possible as an athlete.

Ethel Smith also continued to compete after returning home. In February 1929, she finished third in the 50 yards dash at the Millrose Games, inches behind Jane Bell. Later that month, at the first National Indoor Track Championships in Toronto, she tripped at the finish of the 60 yards sprint, severely injuring her knee. Alex Gibb came up to her right after and told her that she must walk off the track. When Ethel replied that her knee was hurt quite badly, Alex said, "If it's possible, walk off this . . . [track] because they don't want women competing in sports and if you get hurt they will say, 'There you are.'" So Ethel walked off the track, despite the pain. "There were times you had to show that you had it in you," she said. Her final competition was the Ladies' Ontario Track-and-Field Championships in August, where she won the 60 yards sprint.

Canada's Sports Hall of Fame

Ethel Smith in her Norway Avenue home a year before she died, holding her gold and bronze medals from the Amsterdam Olympics.

Although her career as a track athlete was over, she carried the memories of Amsterdam for the rest of her life. "It always surprises me how many people remember the 1928 Olympics and how well Canada did," she said, years afterwards. "I can still see how close Myrtle came to stepping over the line in the relay race."

A year before she died in 1979, an interviewer asked Ethel about her life in sports and if she believed athletes of today were spoiled. She replied they were given so much that it affected their incentive. To succeed, she said, they had to possess the will to run and to work for everything they got. She was then asked to imagine she was sixteen again. Would she be training for the 1980 Olympics? "Yes I would," she replied, without hesitation. "Sure I would. If I was 16 . . . oh boy! Yes, I would. My heart is still in it."

Ethel Smith is one of only four Canadian female athletes to win two medals in track and field at a single Olympic Games. The others are Bobbie Rosenfeld in 1928, Hilda Strike in 1932, and Marita Payne in 1984.

★

Don McGowan

Myrtle Cook in the early 1960s being interviewed by her son, Don McGowan.

For several months after the Olympics, Myrtle Cook tried to meet the winner of the Olympic 100 meters, Elizabeth Robinson, to decide who was the fastest woman in the world. Her attempts were unsuccessful and she never faced Robinson again. The unanswered question nagged, causing Myrtle to forever ponder her disqualification at the Olympics. "There's no question this bugged her," her son said. "There's no question she would have . . . liked another shot at it. Unlike some athletes, she couldn't entirely turn the page on that day in Amsterdam."

In April 1929, Myrtle moved to Montreal to write about women's sports for the *Montreal Daily Star*. "Girls in sport, this is your column!" she announced. It marked the beginning of a forty-four-year association with the newspaper.

Not content merely to write about sport, Myrtle organized the Montreal Major Ladies' Softball League and the Montreal Major Ladies' Hockey League. To encourage girls' track and field, she formed a branch of the Canadian Ladies' Athletic Club (CLAC), and became its director of athletics. She did all of this while continuing to compete. By 1931, no longer fast enough, she retired from racing. She then spent much of her time coaching athletes she had recruited for the CLAC. One of them, Hilda Strike, won two silver medals at the 1932 Olympic Games in Los Angeles.

During the Second World War, Myrtle was the track coach for the army, navy, and air force bases in the Montreal area, training men and women for interservice competition. She attributed this to her Olympic experience. "The gold medal didn't mean a lot in its intrinsic value," she said, "but the thing that it represented meant an awful lot to me, and I was always hoping that I could help some other girl or boy. And some of my boys got [athletic] scholarships. Now that is a rewarding thing and that all started from the fact that I won a gold medal and felt that I could pass on the information that I had."

Throughout her long newspaper career, Myrtle had a special interest in the Olympics, and covered almost all of them when she worked for the *Star*. Like Bobbie Rosenfeld, she was dismayed by the failure of Canada's athletes to repeat their success in Amsterdam. After the Canadian women's athletic team won only two bronze medals at the 1936 Berlin Olympics, she lamented that Canada was either standing still, or content merely to shuffle along in track and field, while other countries seemed to be moving ahead. Nor could she abide Olympic athletes who turned in a mediocre performance and blamed everyone but themselves for their results. After the 1956 Melbourne Olympics, where the Canadian track-and-field team won no medals, she put it down to the refusal of many athletes to make sacrifices to attain their goal. "Most of them have to be pampered, cajoled, and given everything on a silver platter," she remarked.

Although her disqualification in the 100 meters in Amsterdam lingered until her death in 1985, Myrtle found consolation in the good memories of the relay victory and the world's championship. "She always talked about what a happy time it was," her son recalled. "That was the greatest moment. Nothing will ever replace that kind of 'salad days' experience."

★

Ethel Catherwood returned from Amsterdam having achieved everything she had set out to do. The Saskatoon Lily soon discovered the spotlight shone even brighter after the Olympic Games. The adulation she received in Saskatoon was impressive, but in Toronto the attention was fervent and invasive. Crowds followed her everywhere. She could walk into any store and they would give her anything she wanted. Joe Griffiths recalled that a church was holding a bazaar to raise money and asked Ethel to put in an appearance. She agreed and the throng was so great that they took in enough money to wipe out their debt. A suggestion that she sell poppies at the corner of King and Yonge Streets was abandoned because police would be needed to control the multitude.

Ethel resented her loss of privacy. "We used to go to the show at night and she would be striking," Jane said. "Everybody would be looking at her and she was so self-conscious about it." Twenty years later, another Olympic champion, Barbara Ann Scott, described what Ethel likely endured. "Sometimes I feel like a freak or a monkey in a zoo," she said. "I often seem to be something people have conjured up in their minds, something they want to believe I am, something a little bit better than perfect – which no one can be."

What many failed to realize was, Ethel had changed. No longer was she the athlete who had journeyed to Amsterdam determined to win a world title. She was now the Olympic champion and world record holder – the best there was. What more remained? Nothing, it seemed. For the next three years, she competed sporadically, her enthusiasm for high-jumping turned cold. She missed the Canadian Women's Track-and-Field Championships in 1929 because of a training injury, but participated the next year, winning both the high jump and javelin throw. Yet her performances were undistinguished. The lack of competition and injuries finally caught up with her at Wetaskiwin, Alberta, in 1931 at the Canadian Women's Track-and-Field Championships. An astonished audience of 3,000 watched as she failed three times to clear the bar at 4 feet 9 inches and left the field. She finished third, the first time in her career she had been beaten. But the Saskatoon Lily was undismayed. "What do a couple of titles matter," she said. "I still hold the record."

Photo #LH 3476, courtesy of the Saskatoon Public Library – Local History Room

Ethel Catherwood in 1936.

In December it was revealed she had been secretly married for two years to a Toronto bank clerk and was in Reno, Nevada, seeking a divorce. For a public who idolized her, the concealed marriage and its failure were two more shattered illusions in a Depression full of them. The sensationalist manner in which the story was covered by the newspapers had its effects. Her relationship with the press, not always the best, was irreparably broken. Teddy Oke deplored the publicity that had come on her like a flood. "I'm afraid this may hurt her terribly," he said, adding that Toronto was "the smallest big town on the American continent" because of the way it was riding her. She never returned to Canada: Remarrying, she spent the rest of her life in the United States. Her tenuous connection with the other members of the Olympic team ended.

In 1977, a *Toronto Star* reporter traced her to Palo Alto, California. He asked her about her athletic feats, and she told him she had completely forgotten about them and had given away all her medals and trophies. Moreover, she had no interest in sport, and wished some Canadian girl would jump 17 feet, then everyone would leave her alone. Her high-jump record, set in Halifax in 1928, stood until 1954. She died in 1987 and remains the only female track-and-field athlete to win an individual gold medal for Canada at a Summer Olympics.

In September 1928, Jane Bell began her studies at the Margaret Eaton School. She continued to compete for the Parkdale Ladies' Athletic Club and was one of its best track-and-field athletes. At the Canadian Women's Track-and-Field Championships in Montreal in 1929, she matched her Canadian record in the 60 yards hurdles and won the javelin and the baseball throw. That same year, she was the winner of both the 60 and 100 yards hurdles at the Ontario ladies' championship meet.

Graduating from Margaret Eaton in 1930, Jane worked as a physical education instructor at the Guelph YWCA. Because she received payment for her job, she was deemed a professional and ineligible for the 1932 Olympics. But

Judy McNaughton

Even in old age, Jane Bell shows the irrepressible spirit that typified her life. "Calamity Jane" was still ready for an adventure.

she didn't care. "I didn't want to compete to that degree anymore," she said. "I had given up everything. I had reached everything I had ever wanted to do. I just wanted to have fun."

She stayed in touch with Bobbie and Ethel Smith. At the opening of Canada's Sports Hall of Fame in Toronto in 1955, she and Ethel came upon a group of young girls examining the picture of the relay team taken right after their victory in Amsterdam. Overhearing one of the girls say, "It's a good job they can do something because they're not good looking at all," Jane and Ethel gave each other a poke. Jane walked up to the group, pointed to herself in the photograph, and said, "Don't you think she's not bad looking?" One replied, "She's better than the rest, but she's no beauty either." They looked right at Jane without realizing who she was.

When Bobbie died in 1969, Jane felt it keenly. For she was the glue that held the relay team together. Whenever she was honored for something, she always mentioned the others. Now that Bobbie was gone and Myrtle in Montreal, Jane and Ethel represented the squad.

For the longest time after the Olympics, Jane was modest about her accomplishment. Gradually, she recognized its significance. "I love when people say, 'Do you know that Jane has an Olympic medal?'" she said. "It just means so much more now than actually it did in the beginning." She also realized, as an Olympic champion, she belonged to a select group of athletes who shared a special relationship. "When that flag goes up [at the Olympics] and whoever's the winner," she said, "they feel exactly like I felt. . . ."

Despite becoming an American citizen, Jane stayed a passionate Canadian at heart all her life, fiercely loyal to her native country. She cheered Canadian athletes at every Olympics, and eventually donated her Olympic gold medal to Canada's Sports Hall of Fame. When she died in 1998, she was the last of that distinctive band of Canadian female Olympians known as the "Matchless Six." Her passing marked the end of a remarkable chapter in women's sport.

Prior to the Los Angeles Olympics in 1932, Myrtle Cook observed that the girls who wore the Maple Leaf at these Games would owe their presence to the wonderful performances and excellent conduct of the first Canadian women's Olympic team. "Canada's 'matchless six' were overwhelmingly outnumbered," she said, "but brought back the world's championship for women, a splendid example for subsequent teams." Little did Myrtle know that their title as the "Matchless Six" would be apt. For the standard they set at the 1928 Olympiad has been unequalled by a team of Canadian women athletes since. "We accomplished what we set out to do," Jane said. "We were disciplined, we learned to make the sacrifice, and we never, ever gave up." By their achievements, they showed that athletics for women belonged at the Olympics and that gender should no longer be a criterion for participation. The success of this small band of six changed the face of the Olympic Games forever.

Acknowledgments

A book such as this is not the product of one person, but of many. The following people and institutions provided valuable information, research material, photographs, and support. Thank you to Jane Bell Doane, the last surviving member of the "Matchless Six," for her reflections about the women's team and the Amsterdam Olympics; her children, Judy McNaughton and John Walker, and her sister, Marion Helmer, for their insights; Don McGowan for material and recollections of his mother, Myrtle Cook; Ethel Berman, who answered questions about her sister, Bobbie Rosenfeld, and Jean McCann for information about Bobbie's years in Barrie; Dorothy Varley for her remembrances of her older sister, Ethel Smith; Barbara Howard for information about her aunt, Jean Thompson; Bob Florence of the Saskatoon *Star Phoenix* for his diligent work of researching Ethel Catherwood; Doreen Stokes for photographs and stories of her mother, Rosa Grosse; Edna Robinson, Bobby Robinson's daughter, for photographs; Frankie Davies, Eva Dawes, and, especially, Flo Taylor for their memories of girls' sports in Toronto during the 1920s; the City of Toronto Archives, the National Archives, the Canadian Olympic Committee, and the Saskatoon Public Library – Local History Room for photographs; Canada's Sports Hall of Fame, particularly Alan Stewart, executive director, for his help in making this book a reality, and his untiring efforts to save the Hall of Fame; my colleagues and students at Frontenac Secondary School, Kingston, for their encouragement, and the classes from other schools who enjoyed hearing the story of the "Matchless Six;" the incredible group of historians who taught at Trent University during its early years, especially Professor Alan Wilson, who fostered my love of history and research; finally, Joanne for her patience and good humor in sharing her husband with six women who were the first to compete at a Summer Olympics.

Index